Life after care

The experiences of young people from different ethnic groups

Ravinder Barn, Linda Andrew and Nadia Mantovani

JOSEPH ROWNTREE
FOUNDATION

The **Joseph Rowntree Foundation** has supported this project as part of its programme of research and innovative development projects, which it hopes will be of value to policy makers, practitioners and service users. The facts presented and views expressed in this report are, however, those of the authors and not necessarily those of the Foundation.

Joseph Rowntree Foundation
The Homestead
40 Water End
York YO30 6WP
Website: www.jrf.org.uk

About the authors

Ravinder Barn is Professor of Social Policy and Social Work at Royal Holloway, University of London.

Linda Andrew is a freelance consultant, trainer and researcher.

Nadia Mantovani was a researcher on the study. She is currently a PhD student at Royal Holloway, University of London, studying early childbearing amongst young people in care from black minority ethnic groups.

First published 2005 by the Joseph Rowntree Foundation

ISBN 1 85935 191 3   (paperback)
ISBN 1 85935 192 1   (pdf: available at www.jrf.org.uk)

A CIP catalogue record for this report is available from the British Library.

Cover design by Adkins Design

Prepared and printed by:
York Publishing Services Ltd
64 Hallfield Road
Layerthorpe
York YO31 7ZQ
Tel: 01904 430033;   Fax: 01904 430868;   Website: www.yps-publishing.co.uk

Further copies of this report, or any other JRF publication, can be obtained either from the JRF website (www.jrf.org.uk/bookshop/) or from our distributor, York Publishing Services Ltd, at the above address.

They can talk and do all the things ... but until they adjust their system to fit the needs of the people that need them, we will never be perfect or right. It may suit some people because they might get on with someone they bond with or their foster family but what about those ones that can't bond with nobody.
(Care Leaver)

Contents

Acknowledgements

We would like to express our thanks to the young people and social work professionals who participated in this study. It was their responsiveness, drive and dedication that provided us with the material with which to write this report. We hope that we have done justice to their accounts.

The advisory group (Nina Biehal, Bob Broad, Ronny Flynn, Martin Hazlehurst, Michael Henry, Amina Begum) were superb in their ongoing support and commitment to this study. Thank you to you all.

We would also like to acknowledge the help and assistance given by Linda Ince to this study during the early stages of this work.

Finally, the Joseph Rowntree Foundation (and, in particular, Charlie Lloyd, Principal Research Fellow) deserve a special mention. This study was made possible with their vision and understanding about the need for research in this hitherto neglected area.

Summary

This research study reports on the findings arising from a sample comprising 261 care leavers from across England. With its focus on race and ethnicity involving a large group of minority ethnic young people (116), the study makes an important and original contribution.

The research study was conducted at a time when the Children (Leaving Care) Act 2000 was in the early stages of its implementation. It should be recognised that this study did not set out to provide an assessment of developments post the C(LC)A. Given the chronic dearth of literature concerning minority ethnic care leavers, the key contribution of this study is to document the perceptions, needs and concerns of minority ethnic care leavers. However, a broad perspective has been adopted to also include the perceptions and experiences of white care leavers, and those of service providers. It is hoped that the findings arising from this piece of work will be of use in the planning and provision of services.

A total of six local authority social services departments participated in the study. The findings document some interesting parallels between young people from different ethnic groups. The overwhelming finding of this study is that the profile of need across different ethnic groups shows many similarities. It is evident that the in-care experience plays an important role in the subsequent life opportunities of young people. The overall general positive experiences of Asian and African young people, and the relative deprivation and disadvantage experienced by white, mixed parentage and Caribbean young people, provide evidence of the complexity of ethnicity and multiple disadvantage faced by care leavers.

1 Introduction

There is much research evidence documenting the marginalisation and social exclusion of care leavers in a range of areas concerning transition to adulthood and independence. However, because of a lack of focus on the needs and concerns of minority ethnic care leavers, there is a serious gap in our knowledge and understanding about the situation of these youngsters. The impetus for this study, therefore, came from a serious paucity of research evidence into preparation and after-care experiences of minority ethnic care leavers.

This study documents the findings concerning the post-care experiences of 261 minority ethnic and white young people in England. A number of key areas including education, employment and training, housing and homelessness, crime and delinquency, substance misuse, identity, and preparation and after-care support are explored. The views and experiences of social work professionals are also provided to present a contrasting picture of the process of preparation for leaving care and after care.

Background

Since the mid 1970s, a distinct body of small-scale studies has raised our awareness of the range of problems faced by young people leaving care and has highlighted the relationship between the 'in-care' and 'post-care' experience. However, a plethora of significant studies about leaving care have failed to pay adequate attention to outcomes for minority ethnic young people leaving local authority care.

The over-representation of minority ethnic young people in the care system (particularly those of African Caribbean and mixed parentage background) and the likelihood of these youngsters spending lengthy periods in care has been reported by empirical research studies for some time, and is now evident from the official government statistics (Bebbington and Miles, 1989; Rowe *et al.*, 1989; Barn, 1993, 2005; Barn *et al.,* 1997). Moreover, minority ethnic young people are disproportionately represented among those leaving care between the ages of 16 and 18.

Early British studies have noted the diversity of the care experience, as well as variable levels of preparation (Godek, 1977; Kahan, 1979; Burgess, 1981; Stein and Carey, 1986; Randall, 1989). It is argued that, although many young people have valued the time spent in public care, the local authority as a corporate parent has not always provided sufficient compensation for poor pre-care experiences and may have created further problems (Wade, 2003). It has been documented that poor levels of educational attainment and high levels of unemployment, poverty and isolation were factors that featured in the lives of many young people on leaving care. It was significant that children who were looked after moved frequently from one placement to another, thus disrupting their education, and relationship with relatives and friends. Many had lost contact with family or contact was generally poor. Stein and Carey (1986) show that there was a growing link in these early years between such factors as constant movement, loss of contact, high unemployment and unsatisfactory accommodation. What was unclear during these years was how young people dealt with these problems and what happened to them post leaving care.

Other problems associated with leaving care include the fact that young people are expected to leave care at a much earlier age than young people in the general population (Biehal, *et al.*, 1992; Garnett, 1992). A majority will move to independent living before the age of 18 compared to fewer than one in ten of their peers (Jones, 1995). Wade (2003) argues that, while some young people are attracted to the idea of independence and push to leave, moving on is also influenced by a number of push factors, including placement breakdown, limitations in the supply of placements, problems in managing challenging behaviour and traditional expectations about the right time to leave.

Few studies have endeavoured to make pertinent comparisons between minority ethnic and white young people, or for that matter focus exclusively on minority ethnic young people leaving care (Biehal *et al.*, 1995; Stein and Wade, 1999). Small (1984) and ABSWAP (1983) were some of the first commentators to note the ill effects of institutional care on minority ethnic children and young people. A conference report by minority ethnic young people who had spent a large part of their life in the care system documented that racism, and a lack of cultural knowledge affected their confidence and self-esteem, compounding their leaving-care experience (BIC, 1984). This was followed by a small-scale survey by First Key in 1987, which found that transracial placements or placements in predominantly white areas left minority ethnic young people confused about their cultural identity.

The most recent piece of work documenting the experiences of minority ethnic care leavers was produced by Ince (1998) in a qualitative study of ten black care leavers. Ince suggests that a process of 'identity stripping' is being experienced by minority ethnic young people who are looked after and emphasises that, without a positive sense of identity, these young people find it extremely difficult to forge links with their communities and make a successful transition to adulthood.

The policy framework

The Children Act (1989) provided the general legal framework for care leavers. However, while it gave local authorities the power to support care leavers, it imposed few duties. Furthermore, various studies have highlighted the poor outcomes for young people leaving care and have argued that insufficient funding from central government for the Children Act resulted in significant geographical disparity in provision (Utting, 1991; First Key, 1992; Garnett, 1992; Broad, 1994).

Our study was conducted at a time of change in the provision of leaving care, namely the introduction of the Children (Leaving Care) Act 2000, which aims to address the deficiencies inherent in previous legislation. Before detailing the main provisions of the C(LC)A it is important to consider the broader policy framework within which this legislation exists.

Quality Protects programme

The Quality Protects programme (QP) launched by the Department of Health (DoH) in 1998, was designed to deliver the Government's plans for improving the outcomes and life chances for children and young people in care and other children in need. The initiative has aimed to reduce the numbers of young people leaving care too early, as well as to increase levels of advice, assistance and support offered to care leavers. Local authorities are required to evidence clear indicators in relation to providing support for young people and in developing a clear pathway to independence.

Along with national objectives, QP has set out clear outcomes and targets for local authorities. These include:

> [Objective 5:] ... to ensure that young persons leaving care, as they enter adulthood are not isolated and participate socially and economically as citizens.
> (DoH, 1998)

In addition, there are sub-objectives that aim to increase the number of care leavers in education, training or employment, as well as those in contact with social services and who have suitable accommodation. The Government has provided a ring-fenced budget for meeting QP objectives, while all local authorities must produce annual Management Action Plans (MAPs), highlighting how they intend to achieve these objectives.

Within the context of the public policy agenda, the relevance of the QP initiative cannot be overstated. Its emphasis on the responsibility of the corporate parent and insistence that local authorities produce evidence of measured outcomes will ensure that social services departments are scrutinised with more rigour and precision than was previously the case. However, in the absence of any specific national objectives for black young people, early evidence from the year one evaluation of MAPs, produced by the DoH in 1999, showed inconsistent information on the minority ethnic population (DoH, 1999a). Consequently, at a national level, it was difficult to establish what work had taken place to plan services that resonate with the needs of minority ethnic care leavers.

The DoH responded to this gap by establishing a QP projects team in 1999 to improve services for minority ethnic children and their families, with a specific remit to monitor practice at a local level and develop four demonstration projects for the purpose of producing best practice guidance documents.

Connexions strategy

The Government's Connexions strategy is an integrated advice, guidance and personal development service for all 13–19 year olds in England. While the strategy is aimed at all young people, it gives priority to those most at risk of underachievement and social exclusion. Social services have a particularly important role with the Connexions scheme in relation to meeting the Quality Protects education targets, and working with parents and carers of children looked after and care leavers. The introduction of a flexible and diverse school curriculum, an apprenticeship scheme, targeted financial support in education and a personal adviser are recognised as key developments in working with young people at risk of disaffection (DfEE, 2001). The personal advisers, who are drawn from a range of agencies (youth service, youth offending teams and social workers), will be located in a variety of settings such as schools and FE colleges. Their role in befriending and supporting individual young people in education and employment, and in overcoming the fragmentation of services, will be challenging but necessary (Pierson, 2002).

The Children (Leaving Care) Act 2000

The Children (Leaving Care) Act provides a new framework for leaving care services. Its purpose is to delay transitions, improve preparation, planning and consistency of support for young people, and strengthen arrangements for financial assistance (Wade, 2003). The main provisions of the Act, which came into force on 1 October 2001, include the new requirement to assess and meet the needs of care leavers, provide personal advisers and develop pathway planning for young people up to the age of 21 (or beyond if continuing in education).

The requirement for a pathway plan under the Children (Leaving Care) Act is to enable the local authority to be a better corporate parent in meeting the essential needs of a care leaver. It is stipulated that each care leaver should have a pathway plan in which they should be extensively involved and that the plan should look ahead at least to the young person's 21st birthday. The plan should build on and extend the aspects covered in the *Framework for the Assessment of Children in Need* (DoH, 2000b), for example, future education, health needs and supporting family relationships. It is required that social services work jointly with housing agencies to carefully assess young people's accommodation needs before they leave care. Sources of income and avenues to employment must also be considered. Pathway planning is envisaged as a multi-agency task, co-ordinated by the personal adviser, and subject to regular review. Regulations and guidance specify the core areas that must be addressed (DoH, 2001a).

Aims of study

Given the weight of previous evidence pointing to poor outcomes for care leavers and the relative dearth of literature concerning minority ethnic young people, one of the key aims of this study was to explore the impact of ethnicity on social exclusion experienced by care leavers.

We were interested in exploring the outcome of young people in a range of areas such as education, housing, employment and training. Moreover, we wished to ascertain their views and experiences in order to develop a picture of the nature and extent to which young people felt supported to become active citizens. The perceptions of social work professionals (senior managers and practitioners) were also explored. A particular emphasis was placed on perceived needs and concerns, and support levels.

Methods of study

The study approach was both quantitative and qualitative in nature. A range of methods such as demographic profile questionnaire, semi-structured interview and focus group were employed to elicit information, and to ascertain the views and experiences of young people.

The study was carried out in six local authority social services departments in London, and central and northern England. Both the quantitative and qualitative research was conducted in the Leaving Care Teams of these authorities. Pseudonyms have been employed throughout this report to maintain anonymity.

Quantitative methods

A quantitative questionnaire, designed to elicit profile data and an understanding of the patterns and outcomes of care leavers, generated a sample of 261 respondents.

The questionnaire was targeted at all those involved with Leaving Care Teams in our chosen research sites. The response rate varied geographically and in terms of ethnicity. Our three London authorities generated the majority of minority ethnic respondents. However, the overall response rate was lower in the London authorities compared to those outside. Only about a quarter of the care leavers responded to our survey questionnaire in London compared to almost two-fifths in Heatherton and Leyford, and almost 50 per cent in Petersfield. It is important to note that, while our findings may be of interest and use in understanding the needs and concerns of care leavers, they are nevertheless based on young people who were in contact with social services Leaving Care Teams. The circumstances of those not involved with social services may well be very different and perhaps more difficult.

The quantitative demographic questionnaire included questions on age, gender, ethnic background, placement, length of time in care, family contact, educational status, school exclusion, sex education, employment, housing/homelessness, substance misuse, social networks and teenage parenthood.

The questionnaire was piloted and a consultation exercise was also carried out to explore young people's views and reactions to the kind of questions included in the study. Appropriate amendments were made following these initiatives. Every effort was made to ensure that the questionnaire would engage young people. Thus, issues around rapport, applicability and sensitivity were carefully explored.

Qualitative methods

Young people
A semi-structured interview schedule and a topic guide for focus group discussions (FGD) were devised to explore the views and experiences of young people. The major areas explored included preparation for leaving care, experiences since leaving care, housing/homelessness, education/employment/income, crime, neighbourhood, substance misuse, relationships, prejudice/discrimination and identity.

A purposive sampling approach was adopted to obtain a good cross-representation of the quantitative sample to include adequate numbers of minority ethnic young people, and also to maintain a reasonable gender balance. Given the significant number of teenage mothers in our sample (55), it was decided to actively include these young people in the qualitative study to explore their particular needs and concerns.

Our qualitative sample included 36 young people (16 male, 20 female) from different ethnic groupings. This amounted to 11 African Caribbeans, eight Africans, three Asians, ten mixed parentage and four white.

Although we have been successful in obtaining extremely rich qualitative accounts from a number of willing young people, it needs to be recognised that attempting to elicit the views of a vulnerable and highly mobile population can be extremely challenging. It is crucial that the views and experiences of care leavers are documented and taken into account by service agencies in the development of policy, practice and provision.

Professionals

Semi-structured interviews were carried out with 13 managers and practitioners located in the Leaving Care Teams in our chosen research sites. The interviews focused on a number of areas including support and preparation for leaving care, ethnic monitoring and statistical databases, the Leaving Care Act and its implementation, the needs of minority ethnic care leavers, equal opportunities policies and ethnicity matching in caseload allocation.

Data analysis

Quantitative data were analysed using conventional, descriptive statistics. Analysis was performed with the SPSS package. Chi-square tests were performed to look for in-group and between-group differences. Analysis of variance (ANOVA), t test and Hierarchical Loglinear analysis were undertaken to assess both how much variation could be attributed to various sources and their interaction effects.

Tape-recorded interviews were transcribed verbatim. A thematic analysis using the Grounded Theory approach was used by the research team to identify the emerging and comparative themes under each topic area (Glaser and Strauss, 1967; Glaser, 2002).

The structure of the report

The report is structured to provide a good overall understanding of the key findings from the study.

Chapter 2 highlights the profile of the research sites to provide a context for understanding the localities in which the young people were living. Background details on the socio-economic circumstances of the area, and the demographic statistics on the ethnic composition of the local population and the looked-after and care-leaver population are provided.

In Chapter 3, we focus on the general demographic and care career profile of the young people in our study. A breakdown of key variables such as age, ethnicity, gender, length of time in care and placement experiences is given.

Chapter 4 documents the transition of young people from the world of care to that of employment and training. Research findings about the 'in-care' disadvantages arising from this study, in terms of placement disruption and school exclusions, are also highlighted. The experiences of different ethnic groups show a complex picture of heterogeneity and help to move away from simplistic binary notions of black and white.

Chapter 5 focuses on young people's transition to independent living, and explores their views and experiences concerning housing and homelessness.

The route into crime and delinquency for those on the margins of society is well recognised. Chapter 6 highlights findings concerning crime and substance misuse, and explores young people's views and experiences of the neighbourhoods in which they lived.

In Chapter 7, we explore young people's self-perception and their understanding and experience of prejudice and discrimination. This is compared and contrasted with the participating agencies' response to these issues by highlighting the views of practitioners in relation to policy and practice.

Chapter 8 addresses issues and concerns about the key stages of preparation for leaving care and after care. The quantitative and qualitative findings are integrated to demonstrate the important trends as conceptualised by the young people and the social work professionals.

Chapter 9 of the report summarises the major findings, and provides recommendations on salient issues and concerns for the development of appropriate policy and practice.

2 A profile of research sites

This chapter provides a brief profile of the research sites in this study. The study took place in six local authorities (LAs) in England; three were located in London, two in central England and one in the north of England. The names of the localities have been changed as mentioned earlier.

We describe the ethnic composition of the geographical areas, giving an indication of the level of deprivation of these areas, and supply the local authorities' own statistics on the looked-after and the care-leaver populations.

Research sites' profile[1]

The London boroughs have the highest percentage minority ethnic population among their residents. And, specifically, Harwood has a resident population that is predominantly from minority ethnic groups (mainly Asian with less than one-third Indian), Benton has more than a quarter of residents from minority ethnic groups and Crowford more than two-fifths (predominantly Indian). Of the three London LAs considered in this study, Harwood had the highest score in the Index of Deprivation Average of Ward Scores.[2] In 2000, it attained 68 out of 354 wards, compared with Crowford, which scored 107 (out of 354, though in 2000 it fell within the top ten most deprived wards overall in England), and with Benton, which scored 136 (out of 354).

The ethnic structure of the three local authorities (LAs) outside London is predominantly white, with the exception of Petersfield, which has more than a quarter minority ethnic groups (primarily Pakistani) among its residents. The northern city of Leyford had the highest level of deprivation according to the Average of Ward Scores (three out of 354 wards); Heatherton scored 151 (out of 354); and Petersfield attained 91 (out of 354).

Models of after-care provision

It is important to distinguish between two distinct phases in the lives of young people leaving care: preparation for leaving care and after-care provision. Both phases allow young people to make a smooth transition to independence through the acquisition of the necessary skills to master one's life of independence and responsibility. Here we provide an illustration of models of after care adopted in the six LAs observed in this study, highlighting also their use of partnership initiatives such as Quality Protects and Connexions so as to enhance the after care of young people.

The Leaving Care Teams (LCTs) provide a specialist service for young people leaving care, and their remit is to offer care and after-care support to young people aged 16–21. Preparing young people for independence entails individual casework, independence groups and developmental work carried out in partnership with other projects. A Peer Mentoring project is an example of the latter we found in *Benton*. In Benton, the Accommodation and Leaving Care Team consists of nine social workers/ personal advisers, three senior practitioners, a team support manager and a team manager. They also have other workers supporting with benefits, housing and mental health, and two part-time care leavers working as personal advisers, to focus on care leavers who are lacking motivation.

In *Crowford*, an operations manager has overall responsibility for leaving care, and under him/her is a manager who has responsibilities for supervision of staff, currently composed of 15 social workers and a social work assistant. The team offer a 'drop-in centre' to care leavers, employing also two full-time and three part-time youth workers, and an advice worker who is seconded to the YMCA. Teachers are employed as part of the LCT, to work specifically with young people under the borough's Quality Protects initiative. In *Harwood*, they have seven after-care workers/personal advisers, two senior practitioners, a team manager and an administrator. The service has been enhanced by the addition of a floating support worker, a housing adviser and a Connexions and education adviser who are available to meet with young people one day in the week. The services available are provided through an after-care worker.

Outside London, we observe that the services responsible for care leavers change name. In *Leyford*, this service is called Care Leavers' Information and Careers Service consisting of personal advisers. In addition to its after-care remit, the team is also responsible for delivering the Connexions service to children and young people who are looked after in the city. On the other hand, in *Petersfield*, the service is called the 16+ Team, which caters for care leavers and was established by the housing and social services departments. As part of the 16+ Team, a teenage pregnancy worker is now in post, working in partnership with the YMCA, contributing with education and support on sex and relationships matters. In *Heatherton*, the service is divided into three distinct services reflecting different sections of the C(LC)A: a Leaving Care Team attends to the needs of young people leaving care (under section 24); a Community Support Team works with young people at risk of being homeless or abused (section 17); and a Black Specialised Team supports both aforementioned services and focuses on post-16 young people. The latter is a separate service composed of two principal social workers, working within the Leaving Care Team, and a principal social worker. The latter oversees this service and has specific responsibility for those young people from black and dual heritage who are leaving care.

Local statistics on looked-after children and care leavers[3]

The high number of some minority ethnic children in the care system has been documented by researchers for several decades (NCH, 1954; Fitzherbert, 1967; Pinder and Shaw, 1974; Bebbington and Miles, 1989; Barn, 1990). However, whether such high representation is disproportionate compared to their actual numbers in the general population has not been as well documented (Barn, 1993). Since 2001, local authority social services departments have been required to provide annual statistics on the numbers of children and young people 'in need' and on the 'at risk' register, and those 'looked after' (The Children Act 1989; DoH, 2000a). The ethnicity of care leavers is still not available, although the Department of Health plans to provide these data in the near future. It is important to note that, while the Department of Health employs the same ethnic classifications as the census data, not all local authorities have, as yet, begun to follow suit. The definitions of specific ethnic classifications were not always clear. For example, the term 'white' included all white groups in some cases, but only white British in others, while the term 'black' included African, Caribbean and mixed parentage in some cases, but only African and Caribbean in others.

In 2002, there were 59,000 children and young people looked after by local authorities in England. The majority of the youngsters were white. Many of those from a minority ethnic background were described as black, and mixed parentage.

Table 1 shows the looked-after population of the under 18s, divided by ethnic groups, collected at the end of March 2002. We observe that Leyford has by far the highest number of children 'looked after' (1,105). We also notice that the three London LAs have the highest proportion of children looked after from minority ethnic groups, with Harwood having the highest proportion (65 per cent), followed by Benton (56 per cent) and Crowford (54 per cent).

Table 1 Percentage of minority ethnic children 'looked after' in research sites (31 March 2002)

| Research sites | Children looked after under 18 (%) | | | | | |
	Black or black British	Asian or Asian British	Mixed parentage	White	Other	Total
Benton (*n* = 285)	26	6	24	39	5	100
Crowford (*n* = 380)	23	13	18	44	2	100
Harwood (*n* = 360)	46	7	12	35	–	100
Leyford (*n* = 1,105)	10	–	7	82	1	100
Petersfield (*n* = 350)	9	9	7	69	6	100
Heatherton (*n* = 625)	2	–	9	89	–	100

Table 2 highlights the number and percentage of young people, 16 and over, who left care in July 2002. The figures for all three London local authorities show that a high number of young people leaving care are from a minority ethnic background. In Harwood, for instance, an overwhelming 60 per cent of the young people leaving care are described as black, Asian, or mixed parentage. The non-London local authorities (northern and central England) reveal that about a fifth of the young people leaving care are from a minority ethnic background.

Summary

The ethnic composition and the socio-economic profile provided in this chapter show the range of ethnic diversity and social and economic deprivation found in our chosen geographical sites. It is evident that the London boroughs represent greater racial and ethnic diversity than the three authorities located outside London.

The three London LAs have also the highest proportion of minority ethnic groups among their looked-after population. However, while our research sites are not representative of the majority of local authorities found in England, the diversity found in terms of ethnicity and socio-economic circumstances does suggest that the findings of this study will be relevant to a variety of social services across the country.

Table 2 Percentage of minority ethnic care leavers in research sites (2002)

| | Children leaving care 16+ (%, numbers in brackets) | | | | | |
Research sites	Black or black British	Asian or Asian British	Mixed parentage	White	Other	Total
Benton	41 (65)	1 (1)	6 (10)	49 (78)	3 (6)	100 (*n* = 160)
Crowford	26 (42)	9 (14)	10 (16)	55 (89)	–	100 (*n* = 161)
Harwood	48 (70)	5 (7)	7 (10)	34 (50)	6 (9)	100 (*n* = 146)
Leyford	22 (53)	–	–	76 (184)	2 (5)	100 (*n* = 242)
Petersfield	11 (11)	2 (2)	9 (9)	70 (69)	8 (8)	100 (*n* = 99)
Heatherton	10 (14)	3 (4)	9 (13)	78 (111)	–	100 (*n* = 142)

3 Young people's profile and care experience

This chapter details the demographic background of young people who participated in this study. In documenting the care histories of the respondents, the chapter focuses on factors such as 'length of time in care', 'movement between placements', 'type of placements' and 'length of time out of care'. It is hoped that such contextual information will enable the reader to better understand the 'after-care' experiences of young people in this study.

Young people's profile

Young people's ethnic background

Our quantitative sample comprised a total of 261 young people (145 white and 116 minority ethnic). Over two-fifths of the sample group (44 per cent) were of minority ethnic background. The largest minority groupings were those of mixed parentage background (40), African Caribbean (35) and African (29) (see Figure 1). The mixed parentage group comprised 21 Caribbean/white, seven African/white, four Asian/white and eight young people who described their mixed-ethnic background as 'other'. Of the 145 white young people, 127 described themselves as British white, six as white Irish and 12 as white other. The study included 12 Asian young people.

In our study we found that two-thirds of the minority ethnic young people were from the three London authorities. Table 2 in the previous chapter showed that, according to the social services departments' statistics, young people from some minority groups (notably Caribbean and African) were represented in large numbers in the

Figure 1 Ethnic background of young people in sample (*n* = 261)

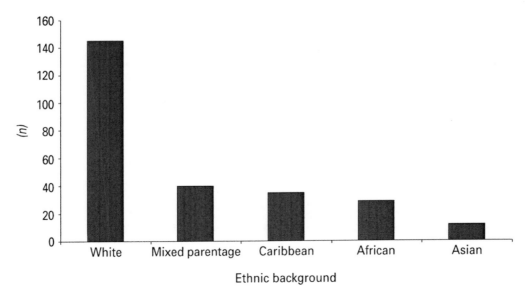

Ethnic background

three London authorities in 2002. Of the 467 care leavers from London, 54 per cent were from black ethnic groups and 46 per cent from white. Our study sample reflects a similar situation, 62 per cent of our London sample were minority ethnic care leavers and 38 per cent were white.

The local authority figures for care leavers from outside London show a smaller proportion of care leavers from minority ethnic groups; 39 per cent compared with 61 per cent of white care leavers. Our study sample reflects a similar picture where 29 per cent of the care leavers were from a minority ethnic background and 71 per cent were white.

While levels of participation in our study cannot be taken as an indicator of young people's involvement with the LCTs, they may help to provide a context for understanding the findings in this study.

Gender

The majority of our respondents were female (57 per cent). There were gender differences within ethnic groups; for example, within the Caribbean group, we had similar numbers of males and females (17 and 18 respectively), while, within the African group, we had more males than females (18 and 11 respectively).

Place of birth

The majority of the respondents were born in Britain (81 per cent). A fifth of our sample were born outside the UK and were likely to be asylum seekers. They were from African countries such as Kenya, Zaire, Eritrea, Somalia, Ethiopia, Nigeria and Sierra Leone; the Balkans such as Kosovo and Albania; and the Baltic region such as Lithuania. Most of the asylum-seeking young people had lived in Britain for about ten years; however, over two-fifths were relatively new and had lived in Britain for two to five years. The highest proportion of this group lived in the three London boroughs.

Religion

Almost half of our sample defined their religious background as Christian (46 per cent). Almost two-fifths (36 per cent) of the young people claimed to belong to no religious group at all. Of the young people who claimed to belong to no religious denomination, the majority were white ($n = 67$), or of mixed parentage background ($n = 17$). Slightly over a tenth of our sample were of Muslim background ($n = 29$), five were Hindus, two Sikhs and six were of 'other' faith. Of the Muslim group, the majority were black Africans.

Age at time of study

Over half of young people were aged between 19 and 20, followed by two-fifths who were between 16 and 18. A small proportion (less than a tenth) were aged 21 or older.

Marital status

Young people were asked whether they were single, in a relationship, married or divorced/separated. The majority of the young people were single (62 per cent), 34 per cent were in a relationship and the remainder were married or divorced. Africans and Caribbeans were more likely than other groups to be single (86 per cent and 80 per cent respectively), compared with about 55 per cent among the other groups.

In addition, we found some variations in the marital status of parents from different ethnic groups. White young parents were more likely to be in a relationship (58 per cent compared with 40 per cent single) than Caribbean and mixed parentage young people who were more likely to be single (64 per cent), and 27 per cent were in a relationship. A study by Berthoud (2000), which examines family formation patterns, has documented variations among ethnic groups and found that Caribbean family formation is characterised by low rates of marriage and high rates of childbearing occurring independently of marriage.

Parenthood

A quarter of the young people as a whole were parents and two-fifths of the young women were mothers. Of these young parents, 94 per cent of the mothers and 77 per cent of the fathers had their first child under the age of 20, either while in care or within two years of leaving care. This is consistent with other studies such as Biehal et al. (1992, 1995) and Garnett (1992).

An analysis of data concerning young women who were parents shows that young women of Caribbean, mixed parentage and white background were more likely to be represented in this group. However, white young women were most likely to be teenage parents ($p < 0.001$). We are unable to make comparison with national statistics on teenage pregnancy among ethnic groups, because of the lack of comprehensive statistics on both live births and abortions by ethnic groups in England. The mother's ethnic group is not recorded if the pregnancy is aborted or during the birth registration (Bluth and Rugh, 2001).

Young people's care careers

Length of timme in care

The vast majority of young people in our sample reported having been in the care system for a long time. As can be seen in Table 3, over a third of the young people had been in care for ten or more years, while a fifth had spent between six and ten years in care. Only five young people reported having been in care for less than a year.

Further analysis of our sample showed that the majority of those who had spent ten or more years in care included mixed parentage (50 per cent), Caribbean (41 per cent) and white (37 per cent) young people. Most of the Asian and African young people had been in care for less than five years.

Age at leaving care

Young people who have been in care start living independently at a much earlier age than other young people in the general population (for example, see Jones, 1995). Starting a household can be a very accelerated transition for care leavers, which entails taking on household responsibilities at a very young age. Managing these types of responsibilities at such a young age can also result in stressful situations, which may be accompanied by much anxiety.

In our study, a third of the young people reported leaving care at 16, over a fifth at 17 and two-fifths at 18. Our findings show that males, on the whole, left care at an older age than females; 47 per cent of males compared with 38 per cent females left care when aged 18.

Across the ethnic groups, white young people leave at an earlier age than the other groups. Our study shows that 41 per cent of white young people left care at the age

Table 3 Years being looked after, by ethnic group (*n* = 231; missing = 30)

Years spent in care	Ethnic background (% in brackets)					
	Caribbean	African	Asian	Mixed parentage	White	Total
Less than one year	1 (3)	–	–	1 (2)	3 (2)	5 (2)
1–2	4 (14)	6 (23)	2 (22)	6 (17)	24 (18)	42 (18)
3–5	8 (28)	9 (35)	4 (45)	5 (14)	30 (23)	56 (24)
6–9	4 (14)	8 (31)	1 (11)	6 (17)	26 (20)	45 (20)
10 or more	12 (41)	3 (11)	2 (22)	18 (50)	48 (37)	83 (36)
Total	29 (100)	26 (100)	9 (100)	36 (100)	131 (100)	231* (100)

* *Twenty-six young people had been in care for more than two years but did not specify the actual length of time. These young people are not included in the above table.*

of 16 compared with 27 per cent Asian, 24 per cent mixed parentage, 14 per cent African and 11 per cent Caribbean. By comparison, we found that the majority of African young people left care at the age of 18 (67 per cent compared with 55 per cent of mixed parentage, 46 per cent of Asian, 44 per cent Caribbean and 31 per cent white). Many of the African young people were asylum seekers and were therefore less likely to have the 'pull' of family and community networks.

One of the main objectives of the C(LC)A 2000 was to discourage the propensity of many local authorities to discharge young people from care too soon, before they are ready for independence. It is now incumbent on local authorities to do their utmost to encourage young people to remain in care until they are 18. Government statistics indicate that, in line with the requirements of the Children (Leaving Care) Act 2000, the number of young people leaving care at 16 declined and there was a rise in the number leaving care at age 18 (DoH, 2003).

Movement in care

Stability and security are essential components for a positive experience in care. Previous research has documented much instability and placement disruption for young people growing up in care (Millham *et al.*, 1986, Berridge and Cleaver, 1987). Sadly, the experiences of some young people in this study were not dissimilar. Almost a fifth had experienced ten or more placements and a quarter had had between four and nine placements.

White and mixed parentage young people suffered most severe placement disruptions compared to the other groups (see Figure 2). Almost half of the young people in these two groups had encountered between five and ten or more placements. By contrast, Asian and African young people had the least disruption when in care; with 67 per cent of Asians experiencing between two and four placements, and 45 per cent of Africans having had only one placement. While the likelihood of less disruption experienced by Asian and Africans can be explained in terms of their late entry into care, it is interesting to note Caribbean young people also experienced least disruption when compared to whites and those of mixed parentage. These differences were significant ($p < 0.000$).

Log linear analysis revealed that there was a significant interaction between the number of placements young people encountered, their ethnic background and their gender ($p > 0.05$). We found that white young women were almost ten times more likely to have experienced severe placement disruption (ten or more placements) compared to other young women in our sample ($n = 27$, compared with one Caribbean woman). They were also more likely than their white male counterparts to experience severe placement disruption (33 per cent white females compared with 20 per cent of white males). White women were also most likely to have had experienced five to nine placements compared with females from other ethnic groups and their white male counterparts. We further analysed the number of years spent in care, whether the young woman was a parent or not and whether she had been placed in a children's home or foster home, but none explained why white young women experienced more disruptions than any other group and also of their male counterparts.

Type of placement in care

Most of the young people in our sample had experienced a range of placements during their stay in care. Eight out of ten had experienced fostering, over half of the group had lived in a children's home and over a tenth had been placed with relatives.

All young people had an equal chance of being placed in the range of placement settings; we found no clear differences in the type of placement across ethnic groups. Some variations existed with regards to kinship placements. Caribbean young people were most likely to experience such placements. Over a fifth of the Caribbean young people had had placements with relatives compared to 15 per cent white, 10 per cent mixed parentage and 3 per cent of African young people. Only one Asian young person had been placed with relatives.

In terms of placements within foster families that reflected the young person's own racial and cultural background, we found that Caribbean and white young people

Figure 2 Total number of placements experienced, by ethnic group (*n* = 257, missing = 4)

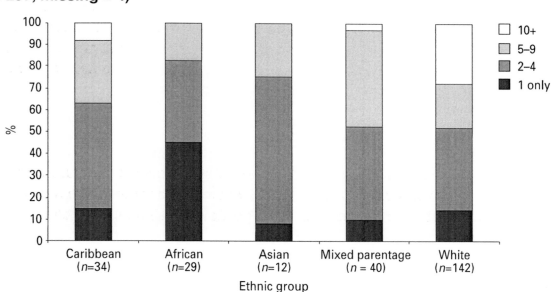

(eight out of ten) were most likely to be placed within such settings. The other groups were dispersed among families from a range of different ethnic backgrounds. Only two-fifths of the Asians, over half of the Africans and just a tenth of the mixed parentage young people were placed in a family that reflected their own racial and cultural background. Mixed parentage young people were generally placed with white (45 per cent) and Caribbean families (34 per cent).

With the exception of one central England local authority (Heatherton), the authorities had been highly successful in placing Caribbean young people in Caribbean or other minority ethnic substitute families. Within Heatherton, almost two-thirds of the Caribbean young people had experienced transracial placements in white families.

There were no clear differences between London and other social services in relation to the placement efforts concerning Asian or mixed parentage children; that is, these youngsters experienced a range of racial and cultural family placements irrespective of geographical location. It seems that the majority of local authorities are successful in placing Caribbean young people within families that reflect their own racial and cultural background; however, this success is still not reflected in the placement of other minority ethnic groups (see Barn, 1993).

Length of time out of care

We were interested to learn about the length of time a young person had been out of care and whether this had had an impact on their post-care circumstances and level of contact with social services. This study shows that those young people who had been discharged recently were more likely to remain in contact with social services. It is likely that their housing and finance needs were greater and therefore their need to remain in contact to receive help and assistance. Findings show that almost two-thirds of our sample comprised young people who had been discharged from care in the previous two years; a quarter left care three or more years ago and one-tenth were being prepared to leave care (and living in semi-independent housing) or had left care within the previous year (see Table 4).

Summary

This chapter offers an illustration of the young people's profile in the study and gives demographic details of the sample. It showed that 55 per cent of young people in the study were from white background and 45 per cent were from minority ethnic groups.

Table 4 Years out of the care system (*n* = 255, missing = 6)

Years out of care	No.	%
Being prepared*	27	11
Less than a year	41	16
One year	66	26
Two years	61	23
Three or more years	60	24

* *These young people were in the process of being prepared but had not been legally discharged from care. They were living in semi-independent accommodation.*

Most of the respondents were British-born. A fifth of the sample were born overseas. The latter group were predominantly unaccompanied asylum seekers. There were more females than males. Two-fifths of the female respondents were young mothers. We found that over a third of the respondents claimed to belong to no religious group at all.

In this chapter we also give details of the care career experiences of young people. We show that mixed parentage and Caribbean were likely to stay in care longer than other groups. We highlighted that white young people tended to leave care at an earlier age than other groups (aged 16) and that African young people left when older (aged 18). It was also revealed that mixed parentage and white young people experienced more placement disruption than other groups. Caribbean young people spent long periods in care, but their placement within a black family may be a protective factor against placement disruption. Our study shows that African and Asian young people came into care as adolescents and experienced the least placement disruption.

4 Education and work

There is much research evidence to show that looked-after young people experience poor educational experiences and attainment compared to their peers (Jackson, 1997). Contributory factors are said to include poor pre-care experiences, school exclusion, educational and behavioural difficulties, poor communication and co-ordination between education and social care agencies, and inadequate support from carers, teachers and social workers (Berridge and Brodie, 1998; Borland *et al.*, 1998; Jackson and Martin, 1998). Encouragingly, some recent research evidence shows that looked-after young people can achieve educational success given the appropriate support structures, including supportive carers, stability at school and in care, and opportunities to develop hobbies and interests (Jackson and Martin, 1998).

Educational attainment is considered to be an important indicator of children's life chances. This chapter documents the transition of young people from the world of care to that of employment and training. Research findings about the 'in-care' disadvantages in terms of placement disruption and school exclusions are also highlighted. The experiences of different ethnic groups show a complex picture of heterogeneity and help to move away from simplistic binary notions of black and white.

Educational experiences

Previous studies have indicated the significantly low levels of educational attainment among care leavers and the impact of this on young people's chances of employment in the competitive labour market (Stein, 1990; Biehal *et al.*, 1995; Britton *et al.*, 2002; Allen, 2003). The National Priorities Guidelines' target for young people leaving care is for 75 per cent of young people leaving care to obtain at least one GCSE with a grade A*–G or a GNVQ (DfEE/DoH, 2000).

It is important to understand the context to interpret the findings arising from our study. The data collected in our study are not a snapshot of care leavers at the point of leaving school. Indeed, over half of our sample were aged between 19 and 20, and almost a tenth were over the age of 21. Thus, young people in our study were not fresh from school. Many had attended further education college to improve their educational status to help them find suitable employment.

Further and higher education

Research evidence shows that minority ethnic young people are likely to go on to further education to compensate for their poor schooling experiences (Berthoud, 1999). Our study shows this to be the case concerning minority ethnic care leavers too. Figure 3 illustrates that two-thirds of our sample were at or had been to college to gain further qualifications since leaving school. Minority ethnic young people

**Figure 3 Attended college after leaving school, by ethnic group
(*n* = 237, missing = 24)**

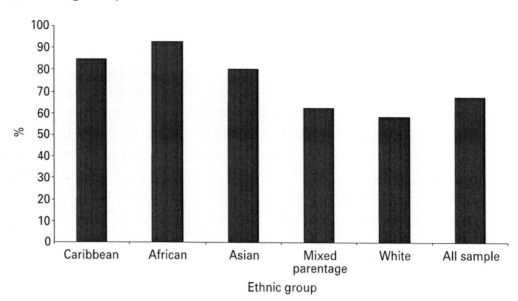

(particularly those of Asian, African and Caribbean background) were considerably more likely to attend college to try to further their studies than white young people. There was little difference between white and mixed parentage young people.

Educational attainment

Our study documents the educational attainment levels of young people at the time of study and not at the time of leaving school. Findings show that 61 per cent of our sample had studied for a GCSE, almost half had studied for a GNVQ and a tenth had studied up to A level. Significantly, 27 per cent did not have any qualifications at all. Of those young people who had indicated actual grade, the figure obtaining GCSE grades A–G fell from 61 to 47 per cent. Thus, only 47 per cent reported achieving at least one GCSE at grades A–G.

Young men were somewhat more likely to be without qualifications than young women (31 per cent compared to 24 per cent). The largest gender difference was found within the Caribbean group where 28 per cent of young males had no qualifications compared with only 6 per cent of the Caribbean young females. It should also be noted that a high proportion of young women who were mothers reported obtaining no qualifications at all. Indeed, of the young parents (*n* = 64), over a third (37 per cent) did not acquire any qualification at all – 47 per cent of white, 30 per cent of mixed parentage and 17 per cent of black young parents reported no qualifications.

An analysis of ethnicity shows that white young people were more likely to be without qualifications than other groups (36 per cent white compared with 26 per cent mixed parentage, 18 per cent Asian, 16 per cent Caribbean and 4 per cent African) (see Figure 4).

Further analysis showed that temporary school exclusion had some effect on the likelihood of educational attainment. Of the white young people who did not obtain any qualifications, 46 per cent had been temporarily excluded from school, compared with 28 per cent who were not excluded from school but who also did not obtain any qualification. There was also evidence of an effect of the number of placements on whether or not white young people had obtained any qualification at all, but its impact was less evident.

Figure 4 shows that Asian, African and Caribbean young people are academically more successful than whites and those of mixed parentage background. Indeed, non-qualification is more pronounced among the latter two groups.

We can see that Asian young people appear to be following traditional academic GCSE and A level qualifications, while Africans and Caribbeans report high involvement in vocational qualifications such as car mechanics and hairdressing.

Figure 4 Educational qualifications, by ethnic group (*n* = 230, missing = 31)

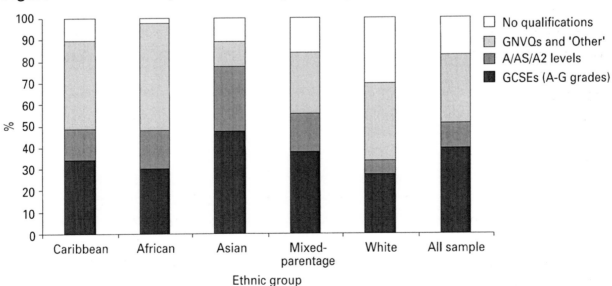

NB The above percentages do not add up to 100 because of multiple responses, that is, young people may have attained GCSEs, but also A levels or GNVQs. To add the GCSE and GNVQ would give a distorted picture, as some young people would be double-counted in the process.

While Caribbean, mixed parentage and white young people all experienced disruption in their education as a consequence of school exclusion, it was white and mixed parentage young people who reported least help from education and social work agencies.

School experiences

Here, we give an account of young people's perceptions of their schooling experience and provide an understanding of some of the difficulties and barriers encountered by the respondents in our sample.

Disruption in education is arguably an important factor in understanding educational attainment levels. For care leavers, such disruption may include placement changes (which can lead to a change in geographical location and school), school exclusion, and personal difficulties. From the previous chapter, we know that white and mixed parentage young people experienced the most disruption in placement. Our findings into education and school exclusion reveal that these two groups together with Caribbean young people are also more likely to be temporarily or permanently excluded from school (DfES, 2002, 2003; Tikly *et al.*, 2004).

Our study shows that Caribbean, mixed parentage, and white young people were more likely to have experienced temporary and/or permanent school exclusion than Asian and African young people (50/41 per cent, 50/21 per cent, 47/37 per cent respectively compared with 18/18 per cent and 26/15 per cent respectively). Also, young men experienced greater temporary and permanent school exclusion than young women (51/43 per cent and 40/24 per cent respectively). Thus, Caribbean, mixed parentage and white young people (predominantly male) were two to three times more likely to report being excluded from school than Asians and Africans (p<0.05).

Of those excluded from school, a high proportion reported not receiving any education at all (44 per cent); just a quarter had home tuition and the remainder went to a special school unit. When excluded from school, mixed parentage and white young people reported receiving less help from their social worker and less help with tuition and learning than any other group, with mixed parentage showing the least level of help.

Some young people believed that they had not been given good educational opportunities and adequate support while in care (Borland *et al.*, 1998). Young people who had been excluded and sent to Pupil Referral Units (PRU), and others who described their own behaviour as unruly and wild, encountered little encouragement and interest from those around them:

I would have liked to be put in a proper school. Because I feel that *[X]* Centre that I was in, that's where all the troublesome kids, that's for kids that have been in trouble with the police, got criminal records, things like that. And it wasn't until then that I actually started getting myself into more trouble. I mean just go in your break and you'd go outside and kids would be smoking weed and that outside … do you know what I mean?
(Lucy, mixed parentage young person, 16, Petersfield)

… they have no boundaries being in care, basically you could do what you wanted. Being a child I hadn't any sense of responsibility, I was pushing boundaries like teenagers do. That was the result of that.
(Joanne, white young person, 21, Leyford)

Many of the young people interviewed were able to recount some positive experiences of their time at school. However, some argued that their care status had affected the dynamic between them and their teachers (Jackson and Sachdev, 2001). Some respondents recalled feeling pitied and/or being picked on:

School was all right I suppose. But it's funny because I was in care … people used to think it's something weird, they used to talk about 'Oh she doesn't have a mum, she doesn't have a dad, she's in care', so it was a horrible experience I suppose. But, I just had to be strong.
(Sarah, African young person, 18, Crowford)

The accounts of some young people revealed that a more active interest from their social worker would have given them some encouragement to do well at school (Jackson, 1997; Francis, 2000). The experience of becoming 'conspicuous' at a time of crisis, such as school exclusion, was expressed by some young people. It was felt that this is where they began to be noticed. However, such attention was often crisis-focused and resulted in little overall support concerning education and/or emotional difficulties:

The only time they took an interest in my schooling was when I got suspended for fighting … That was it, me and her both got suspended and then we got appointed the same social worker and that's when you know, after I went back to school, after a couple of weeks I got put on report and that's when they started noticing. It didn't mean that they done anything special, you know they still omitted to do certain stuff, they just had a meeting every month … asked the teachers about my behaviour but not about my school work, how I was coping with schoolwork, it was about my behaviour.
(Veronica, Caribbean young person, 20, Heatherton)

But the kind of help that I needed *[when he dropped college]* was the kind of help I needed from the start. The fact of having social workers actually sit and talk and take notice, understand what your needs and your problems are, then something's going to be done about it. But if they don't bother they just sit and do what they do and just let you, you're stuck in the same position you started off with. The idea is they're supposed to help you but you're getting nowhere.
(Chris, mixed heritage young person, 19, Petersfield)

Basically ... I would have liked, in the personal development plans, I would have liked them to lay out 'Where do you want to go in the future?... What are your aspirations? Where would you like to go? How can we help you develop as a person?' Because if you're developed as a person then you can live on your own more successfully generally. I would have liked them to ask me ... courses or places to look for courses. But I didn't get none of that.
(Craig, mixed heritage young person, 16, Leyford)

Questions about their experiences of the school curriculum evoked a muted response, even from those who had excelled academically. Friendships and social interaction were the lasting memories that individuals chose to recall. Most respondents held strong views about the value of education and did not feel they had reached anywhere near their potential.

Social services and educational help

The young people who had received help from social services with their studies emphasised that this input had been invaluable:

Yeah I mean they helped me get into college the first time. You know they helped me get into college the second time, which I start soon. So you know they're quite ... you know they do everything, but then they always do anything, I've got another four years with them. They gave me my computer, so that I could do my writing course. It's on loan, but ...
(Focus group, Veronica, Caribbean young woman, 20, Heatherton)

Those at university presented as more settled and financially comfortable than their peers attending further education colleges, and were able to provide a number of examples where the local authority in particular had supported them with their studies. Those respondents who had been displaced from their countries of origin found the education system extremely isolating, yet appeared to cope with this by adopting a disciplined approach to their studies, determined to make the best of any opportunities afforded to them:

> … it's really hard. I mean to be from another country is really hard … cos first of all you have to learn the language. And second you have to know people and know where to go … Now … I'm doing GNVQ intermediate level 2 you know for ICT … It's all going well so far. And I hope I'm going to do this and I'm trying to do some GCSEs and move on and go to university.
> (Defrim, Kosovan young person, 19, Crowford)

Local authorities in these circumstances were described as very supportive. A team manager reinforced this view noting that asylum-seeking young people were highly motivated in taking advantage of the educational opportunities offered to them. However, concern was expressed for some white and Caribbean young people who were not making use of the social services educational budget:

> I think one of the interesting patterns is the funding for further and higher education, we have an educational panel where we decide who we are going to be funding. Sixty-seven per cent of those are actually asylum seekers.
> (White team manager, Benton)

Secondary quantitative data provided by each local authority suggested that, while all the participating research sites had made an effort to work towards the Quality Protects educational targets for care leavers, some had clearly fared better in achieving the cultural shift required to facilitate this process. This was illustrated by the frustrations of a number of young people who noted that, as a result of bureaucracy, requests for educational assistance were often not satisfied or fell short of their needs and expectations:

> I need things for my course like a computer, I need to buy art folders and notebooks … I've spoken to my social worker and I don't know what she's going to do … I just can't afford them with the £42 that they give. I have to eat, I have to dress myself, I have to buy like you know stuff to shave, you know shampoo whatever. So it's really hard.
> (Defrim, Kosovan young person, 19, Crowford)

> I knew that I had the ability to do well and, because they believed in me, they gave me the chance to like to go to … support me through college. I'm now in university becoming like a social worker, training to be a social worker.
> (Focus group, Marcos, mixed heritage young person, 23, Heatherton)

Many of the young people suggested that educational achievement was recognised as a vehicle towards a better quality of life. Those who had left school with few or no qualifications had little belief in their abilities to make improvements. Lack of confidence, apathy and fear of repeating negative school experiences appeared to be holding back some young people:

> I would love to go and get a job, but it's like my maths is atrocious ... I get really panicky if I feel that I can't do something ... I'd love to go to college, but I'm scared of being bullied again. Go through all the trauma and everything just ... how can I say? Just the thought of going, it scares me, scares the life out of me.
> (Kylie, white British young person, 20, Benton)

Employment

The transition from education to employment is at the heart of growing up, as it signals an important shift towards independence, security and adulthood (Bentley and Gurumurthy, 1999). Our findings above indicate that almost three out of ten young people were without any formal qualifications, but that others had obtained a range of qualifications from GCSEs to GNVQs, though a sizeable percentage did not attain a pass grade for GCSEs. The implications of this in securing employment need to be recognised.

We were keen to understand the transition from education to employment. An analysis of young people's employment status reveals that over half of the young people in our sample were unemployed (see Figure 5). Slightly over a fifth were in employment, full or part time. About a tenth were engaged in government training schemes such as New Deal and 16 per cent described their status as 'other' (student, full-time mother or incarcerated in prison).

In a study involving a large sample of care leavers (6,953), Broad (2003) found that 53 per cent of the young people were in education, employment and training (14 per cent in full-time employment, 31 per cent in education and 8 per cent in training). Our study shows some similar trends with 47 per cent of young people in education, employment and training. Those in 'other' were largely in education, and those in part-time jobs were studying and working (see Figure 5).

There were few geographical differences between local authorities. In most areas, about half of the young people were in education, employment and training. However, one of our London authorities (Harwood, 57 per cent) had the highest rate of young people in education, employment and training. This was in sharp contrast to a non-London authority (Heatherton, 40 per cent).

Figure 5 Employment status (*n* = 247, missing = 14)

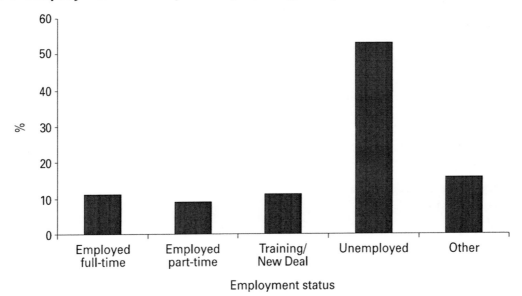

We found that males were more likely to be unemployed than females (57 and 50 per cent respectively), and that females were more likely to work part-time than males (13 and 7 per cent respectively). A higher proportion of males were undertaking a New Deal or training scheme (15 and 7 per cent). An analysis of young parents shows a precarious economic situation with the majority of them being unemployed (70 per cent), and relying on state benefits as a regular source of income (67 per cent) and social services (11 per cent). Research studies have highlighted the limited economic and educational opportunities available to many of the young women who become pregnant at an early age (Phoenix, 1991; Chavalier and Viitanen, 2003).

Although rates of unemployment were high in all groups, we found some ethnic variations. Figure 6 illustrates that Caribbean and white young people reported higher rates of unemployment. Caribbean, African, and Asian care leavers reported little or no involvement in government training schemes compared to white and mixed parentage young people. African young people are more likely to be in full-time or part-time employment. And African, Caribbean and Asian young people in particular reported greater involvement in education. Ethnic variations regarding rates of unemployment and involvement on government training schemes confirm previous studies (DfEE, 1999; Ward, 2000).

It is of concern to observe such high numbers of young people who are unemployed. However, it is encouraging to note that the majority of young people (57 per cent) reported contact or help from the local career services. Given that young people's contact with formal services reduces over time, there is a risk that, unless

Figure 6 Employment status, by ethnic group (*n* = 247, missing = 14)

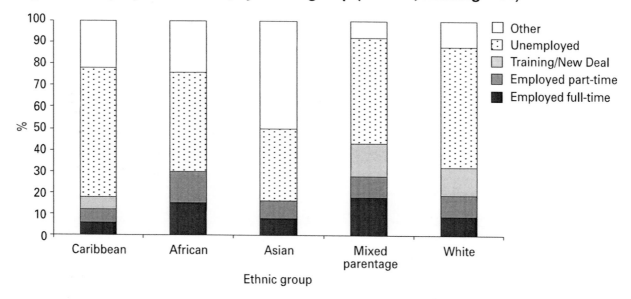

employment and training opportunities are found, these youngsters will join the long-term unemployed.

Young people who were employed were found to be in manual and non-manual occupations. They had unskilled jobs in factories or hotels, or had specialised jobs such as painting, decorating or building. Some worked in retail as shop assistants, cashiers or in customer care. Others worked in catering as waiters, bar tenders or chefs. Some had office jobs as receptionists, personal assistants, administrators, IT specialists. A few young people worked in the care profession, as carers or trainee nurses.

However, their job was not the main source of income for eight out of ten young people. We found that state benefits were the main source of income (44 per cent), followed by social services (24 per cent). Mixed parentage young people were most likely to have state benefits as their main source of income (53 per cent compared with 45 per cent whites, 39 per cent Caribbeans, 36 per cent Africans and 33 per cent Asians). African and Asian groups were most likely to have social services as their main source of support (37 per cent and 33 per cent respectively). This is possibly because a number of them were involved in further and higher education.

Young people who were experiencing financial hardship and were dependent on state benefits exhibited a lack of confidence and a feeling of powerlessness. A lack of adequate qualifications was a major obstacle for many young people:

… most people these days want qualified people to be able to do the job. That's the only problem I'm having, I'd really like to work in a hairdresser's but I have to finish my course first.
(Frances, African young person, 19, Petersfield)

I'd love to work … that would be a dream. To work you know and to pay for my daughter's care and pay for my flat, and just you know being able to do that myself, because I hate being on benefits, it's not a way to live, it really isn't. And that's one message I've got for any person in care … just try your best and never put yourself in a situation, you know never go on benefits, cos it's not worth it.
(Kylie, white British young person, 21, Benton)

Young women emerged as more ambitious and resolute than their male counterparts in education and employment. Some had already identified a clear career trajectory and were confident in this being achieved. They demonstrated clarity, commitment, vision and the ability to take up opportunities:

I normally go down the career centre to look for a job, so when I went down they had a notice on the door saying 'a new deal for families', so I went in and saw a lady called Sarah and she talked me through it, and I looked up the job, she helped me fill in forms for Family Tax Credit … if you find a job that you like and you need training, they train you to get the job and it's quite helpful, and they helped with the babysitting as well, so it was quite helpful for me.
(Frances, African young person, 19, Petersfield)

I'd love to become a certified accountant ... A degree is nothing …
a degree is a foundation.
(Lakisha, African young person, 21, Benton)

I'm going to work in McDonald's or Sainsburys so I can enable myself to make films and do my photography. I want a job with no responsibility … that's what I want while I set myself up. Because I'm not going to be poor and I'm not going to work for anyone.
(Shanice, black British young person, 20, Benton)

Employment played a strong part in their desire for self-actualisation and financial stability. A number of those in part-time employment were also students and were dependent on this income to meet their living expenses, which they viewed as a means to an end. Though, for some young minority ethnic students, part-time work was described as difficult to find because of racism:

> I'm in a place where there's no black people, that in itself you know is like a brick wall … I tried to look for a job that first summer, all my summers were trying to look for a job … I had no employment that first summer, that was when I got into debt, major debt obviously, three months is quite a long time.
> (Lakisha, African young person, 21, Benton)

Although our quantitative data suggest that the majority of young people had been in contact with their local career services, our interviews highlight that, apart from those on government schemes, very few individuals had consulted any other agency to find employment. Just one respondent from Harwood reported using a voluntary organisation that worked specifically to help minority ethnic young people looking for work. There was little awareness of other agencies that could assist them. Given that very few minority ethnic young people (with the exception of mixed parentage) were engaged in government schemes, the lack of possible access routes into employment for these young people is of concern.

A number of Caribbean and mixed parentage young people talked about their experiences of racism and discrimination in employment. Black young women experienced a double jeopardy of racial and sexual discrimination at work. Such experiences caused a great deal of distress, resulted in employment disruption and heralded negative repercussions for future employment opportunities and stability:

> They just called me nigger, stuff like that really. It was really horrible how someone can be so cruel. I'm glad that I did make up stories to go home because if I did stay any longer I know that I would have punched them. And that's what I didn't want to do at the time cos I had enough of that when I was at school.
> (Cecille, mixed heritage young person, 18, Petersfield)

> … they had their eyes on me, because they don't want me to be there, because like you have a child. Every time a child is sick you have to go.
> (Charlene, black Caribbean, 20, Harwood)

Summary

Our study documents important findings concerning education, employment and training of care leavers from different ethnic groups. It is evident that care leavers are a heterogeneous group in terms of pre-care, in-care and post-care experiences. However, there is also a commonality of experience for some groups. Specifically, there is an emergence of three identifiable groups – white and mixed parentage; Caribbean and African; and Asians. While white, mixed parentage and Caribbean young people are similar in terms of experiences of school exclusion, we can see that the Caribbean group then develops a different trajectory. The latter are more likely to go on to further education colleges after leaving school (particularly to study on vocational courses), and are less likely to be without qualifications than white and mixed parentage groups. In this sense, the Caribbean path resembles that of the African young person. The number of Asian young people is small, but we can see that they are most likely to pursue traditional GCSE/A level qualifications. The rates of unemployment for this group are low compared to their counterparts because of their involvement in further and higher education.

Our study shows that young people found it difficult to secure employment without good educational qualifications. Many young people worked in manual and non-manual jobs, and expressed situations of instability and poor pay. In addition, some minority ethnic young people identified racism and sexism at work. Young people were often ill-equipped to deal with these situations.

It is crucial that, if young people are to achieve financial independence and to avoid the poverty trap and the associated social problems, greater efforts are made to focus on their educational potential. This does not necessarily mean an exclusive focus on formal qualifications such as GCSEs and AS/A levels and university education. More effort could be made to identify and support vocational training.

5 Housing and homelessness

Many young people in care experience a series of placement moves and instability. Leaving care to live on their own can herald a positive signal that stability is possible (Biehal and Wade, 1999; Allen, 2003). This chapter focuses on young people's transition to independent living, and explores their views and experiences concerning housing and homelessness.

Accommodation of young people

Local authorities aim to ensure that all young people leaving care are placed in suitable housing in the community. The challenge of securing suitable accommodation for young people is a major concern for housing and social services. Indeed, increasing the amount of appropriate and good accommodation is a clear objective for Government's Quality Protects initiative.

The majority of young people in our study lived in a flat (126) or a house (20). Smaller numbers of young people reported living in other types of accommodation, such as a bedsit or a hostel ($n = 21$, 8 per cent). At a national level, local authorities report that only 7 per cent of young people with whom they are in contact are found in temporary/unsuitable accommodation. Our findings reveal that this figure was as low as 4 per cent in some authorities (namely Benton) and as high as 15 per cent in others (Petersfield). A recent study of 52 leaving-care projects documents that 27 per cent of the projects indicated that accommodation was 'below average' or 'inadequate' (Broad, 2003, p. 17).

Interviews with young people in our study suggest that some of them had experienced homelessness as a consequence of inappropriate housing. Leaving care at an early age was identified as another key factor resulting in difficulties. Policy makers and practitioners were all too aware of these issues:

> ... despite legislation some of the most vulnerable young people leave care earlier ... my view is that this is a resource issue, as they've often exhausted the resources that are available.
> (White senior practitioner, Petersfield)

Many of the young people interviewed informed researchers that they had had very few options in choosing where to live after leaving care. Many felt they had been offered places that were totally unsuitable, yet had been informed that, if they declined to accept, they would be placed at the bottom of the allocations list and would face potential homelessness. It also became apparent that their health and safety was put at risk:

I've had to get heaters ... really old ... it's one of these things that blow black stinky smoke out so I've not put it on, something from the 1950s.
(Anthony, black Caribbean young person, 21, Petersfield)

I'm coming out of care and you're saying to me if I turn that place down you're not going to give me nothing else ... I had to kit the whole place out, it cost me hundreds and hundreds and hundreds of pounds because it was in a bad state ... had an infestation of cockroaches ... The whole place stank, it took me months to get the smell out. There was cockroach droppings all over the linen closet, everything. It was terrible, terrible. It was horrible in there. It was horrible and they *[Social Services]* refused to help me. They said you know if you turn it down that's all you're going to get.
(Kaishia, black British young person, 19, Crowford)

Some young people were placed in hostels, which made them feel isolated and marginalised. They felt they were exposed to behaviours that presented a risk to their safety and protection:

I was living in ... it was kind of a halfway house, but not a halfway house because I'm not a criminal ... So, when I moved in, there was like five young people under 18 and two over 35 ... it was a strange, strange place. So somebody moved out, another person moved in that had just come out of jail and they decided that they weren't really going to try to change their ways and started selling drugs from there and using my name to buy lots of equipment, and I'm blacklisted because of it. It wasn't a good place.
(Shanice, black British young person, 20, Benton)

The variability of service provision was in evidence from the accounts of young people. One asylum seeker from one of our London authorities explained that he had had three different addresses in his 18th year and had been compelled to move because each place had been unsuitable. One dwelling was so poor that it affected his health; when he decided to leave he found himself homeless:

I told them that I can't live in places like that where the water is coming down the walls and it smelt and there was no heating.
(Defrim, Kosovan young person, 19, Crowford)

Given these accounts, we were surprised to discover that this same local authority operated a quota system, which others have clearly benefited from:

> I had four choices, you do an application for a quota flat and four areas
> are offered ... If you don't like the flat in the chosen area, you had to go
> back on the list.
> (Mohammed, African young person, 20, Crowford)

The living arrangements of a few young parents were also a cause for concern.
Some young mothers with small babies were given unsuitable housing located on
higher floors of tower blocks with no lift. One mother felt she did not have the skills to
present her case with authority, and cited this as the reason why she had been
consistently ignored by both the housing and social services departments:

> No, because they give you your flat and you have to take it or you're just
> going to have to wait longer. Because I wouldn't have taken this flat ... I
> love the flat but it's too many flights of stairs for me and I was pregnant
> and then having to carry my pram and my daughter and my shopping up
> the stairs, six flights it's ridiculous. They knew my circumstances and they
> put me up six flights of stairs.
> (Kylie, white British young person, 20, Benton)

The majority of young people lived in areas with a fairly mixed ethnic composition
and seemed satisfied with their local amenities. However, very few respondents
appeared to have integrated well into their local communities, and expressed their
uncertainty and lack of skill and knowledge about achieving this. Others were
content to keep local people at a distance. From the interviews, their sense of
loneliness and isolation was palpable, as they knew very few individuals in the
neighbourhood. For some, the strategy of self-isolation seemed to be a defence
mechanism to avoid getting into the 'wrong crowd':

> I don't know anyone around here at all, and I think that's why I'm staying
> out of trouble and why I'm sorting myself out. But I don't really want to
> know no one around here ... and that's not going against them or
> anything but it's because I don't want to get back into the wrong crowd or
> whatever.
> (Lucy, mixed heritage young person, 16, Petersfield)

In terms of living arrangements, our study highlights that over half of the young
people in our sample lived alone (see Figure 7). African and Caribbean young people
were most likely to be living on their own compared with those of white, Asian and
mixed parentage background. For example, 72 per cent of the African young people
lived alone compared with 40 per cent of those from a mixed parentage background.
Living alone was a difficult and frightening experience for some young people:

… but you know, when you are just not used to actually living by yourself. I'm so used to having been with family or friends or this. So, it was quite difficult to actually be staying by myself. I still, up to now, find it difficult to be in the house alone. It's only now that I'm actually getting to grips with it … I get a bit scared in the night, I sleep with the lights on around the house … I think now I'm getting used to it … bit by bit.
(Semhar, African young person, 19, Harwood)

Not surprisingly, for young people who have grown up in care, only one in ten of our sample reported living with their birth family. We examined the contact young people had with their families and found that almost half had very little or no contact with their birth mother after leaving care, while over two-thirds (68 per cent) had very little or no contact with their birth father. Although there were few ethnic differences between groups, Caribbean young people were more likely to have contact with their birth mother than other groups. The frequency of contact, however, did not mean that young people were likely to live with their birth families.

Homelessness

Previous research has documented that care leavers are significantly represented among the homeless population (Randall, 1989; Smith *et al.*, 1996). Our study shows that over a third of the young people (36 per cent) had experienced homelessness since leaving care. About a fifth had been homeless for a few weeks, while over a tenth had been homeless for several months. A few reported having been homeless for more than a year.

Figure 7 Living arrangements, by ethnic group (*n* = 258, missing = 3)

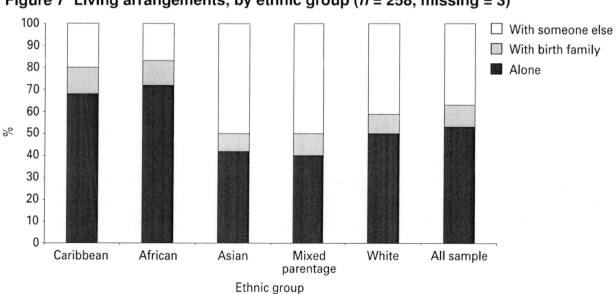

Figure 8 shows the ethnic breakdown of the homeless young people in our study. Compared to the other groups, a higher proportion of white young people had experienced homelessness (43 per cent), though a quarter of them were homeless for a brief period of time. Similar proportions of Asian and mixed parentage young people experienced homelessness, though the latter group for a shorter period. Although African young people were less likely to experience homelessness, those who had become homeless were displaced for a longer period of time. We uncovered a significant relationship between homelessness and the geographical area where the young people lived ($p < 0.005$). Young people from the non-London authorities of Petersfield (53 per cent) and Leyford (52 per cent) reported greater homelessness than others. A comparative figure, which was typical of the other authorities, was 23 per cent for the London borough of Benton. A senior manager from Leyford expressed concern about the standard of housing, which can sometimes be the trigger for homelessness for some young people:

> I have to say some of the standards of accommodation have not been great, and sometimes that's based on the area the youngster wants to live in or whatever.
>
> (White, senior manager, Leyford)

A contributory factor in explaining the higher percentage of white young people among homeless people may be their early departure from care. Our study shows that 57 per cent of those who left care aged 16 were homeless for a period of a few weeks to a year after leaving care.

Figure 8 Homelessness, by ethnic group (n = 258, missing = 3)

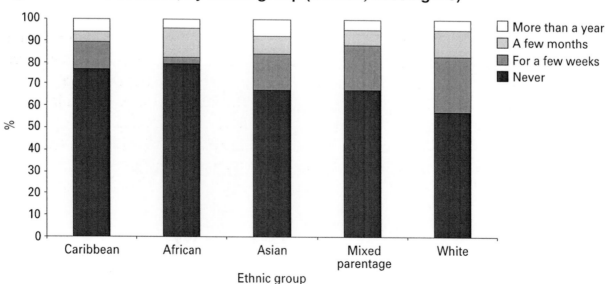

When homeless, young people primarily sought help from friends. Of those who had experienced homelessness, about a fifth had stayed with relatives and the remainder stayed in a homeless shelter, lived on the street or made other arrangements (25, 26 and 16 per cent respectively). In line with previous studies, we can confirm that, with the exception of mixed parentage young people, minority ethnic young people were less likely to sleep rough on the streets and were more likely to have stayed with friends or in a homeless shelter (Davies *et al.*, 1996).

The accounts of young people from our interviews suggest that a number of key factors are influential in young people's poor housing and homelessness experiences. These include early discharge from care at 16 or 17, inadequate preparation for leaving care, unplanned departure from care and unsuitable housing.

While much effort is made to house young people when they leave care, evidence on preparation and after care (see Chapter 8) suggests that more time should be invested in supporting young people to maintain a tenancy. Lack of skill in managing their finances is not the only factor when experiencing rent arrears. Our study suggests that those who were able to negotiate and articulate their difficulties were more likely to recover from such situations. One young person from Heatherton was reluctant to approach social services to ask for help, fearing a negative response. As a consequence, matters deteriorated and he ended up losing his tenancy. In contrast, another young woman from Harwood who was conscious of her poor budgeting skills had managed to negotiate an affordable sum to reduce her arrears and hence keep her flat. Our study shows that young people require consistent support to secure and maintain appropriate accommodation.

Summary

The findings of our study support national figures suggesting that less than a tenth of care leavers are living in temporary/unsuitable housing. While this is an encouraging finding, it is of concern that over a third of the care leavers had experienced homelessness at some stage since leaving care. The lack of skills in maintaining a tenancy and unsuitable housing were key contributory factors resulting in homelessness. White young people were found to be particularly disadvantaged because of their early, and at times unplanned, departure from care.

6 Crime, drugs and neighbourhood

This chapter highlights findings concerning crime, and substance misuse, and explores young people's views and experiences of the neighbourhoods in which they lived.

The previous chapter showed that over half of the young people in our study lived alone. And 21 young people (8 per cent) were found to be living in temporary housing, such as bedsits and hostels, which they described as unsuitable in their interview accounts. Such dissatisfaction was often associated with the neighbourhood. Many young people made a link between drugs, violence and their neighbourhood. Maintaining their distance from others in the neighbourhood was described as an important strategy to keep out of trouble.

Previous research tells us that young people who have been in care are more likely to be involved in criminal activity than their peers in the general population (NCB, 1992). In our quantitative self-completion questionnaire, we regarded it as important to report on not only the nature and extent of criminal activity, but also whether young people themselves had been the victims of crime.

Victims of crime

Our study shows that over two-fifths of the young people reported having been a victim of crime. There were few geographical differences. The most striking difference was between the London borough of Benton (30 per cent) and Heatherton (53 per cent).

While no gender differences in the proportions of young people who had been victims of crime were found, differences existed in the types of crime experienced. For example, seven young women reported rape, attempted rape and domestic violence. Males reported crimes such as mugging, robbery and burglary. Physical violence, racial harassment and bullying were also noted.

In terms of ethnicity, we found that African and Asian young people were least likely to report having been victims of crime, while Caribbean and those of mixed parentage were most likely to do so (see Figure 9).

Criminal activity

Our study shows that almost half of the young people (48 per cent) had engaged in some form of criminal activity. Interestingly, seven out of ten young people in one of our non-London authorities (Petersfield) had been in trouble with the police. In contrast, only two out of ten young people in one of our London authorities had been

Figure 9 Percentage of victims and perpetrators of crime, by ethnic group

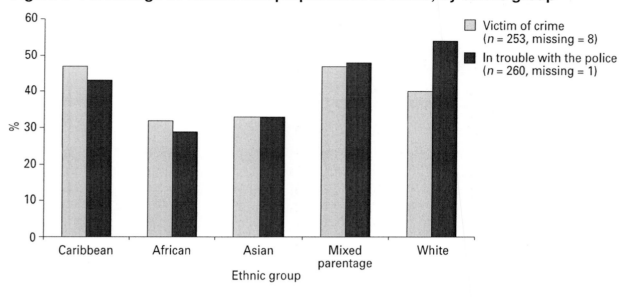

in trouble with the police (Harwood). Ethnic group differences in criminal activity may help to explain geographical disparities.

Our study highlights some ethnic group differences in terms of criminal activity (Figure 9). We found that African and Asian young people were least likely to have been in trouble with the police and white young people were most likely to have been involved in criminal activity (54 per cent). Mixed parentage and Caribbean young people also reported high involvement with the police (48 per cent and 43 per cent respectively).

The types of crimes committed included affray, armed robbery, assault, criminal damage, soliciting, driving without a licence and being arrested for begging. Those with serious criminal activity had been sentenced to prison, while others had been cautioned, or given conditional or absolute discharge.

Eight young people were in prison or in a young offenders' institution at the time of the study.

In our qualitative interviews, we asked young people about their particular neighbourhood and their perceived or real fear of crime and had some contrasting views:

> A hundred per cent safe. Um … I know lots of people. My extended family, like my mum's best friend's kids and my mum's best friend, and then their family.
> (Shanice, black British young person, 20, Benton)

41

It's not that safe because like guns and shit, you get me? Everyone's got a gun, you get me? ... Not right near me but within a mile. It's dangerous, because you walk the street, you can get killed, you can get shot dead. (Robin, mixed heritage young person, 17, Heatherton)

... but in one of the blocks, nearby, somebody put a fire bomb through somebody's door and set their house on fire and the person was inside the house. They didn't die but the person was inside the house and it was at night. On that road there was an armed robbery. Like somebody with a knife and stuff like that on my road. And there was a burglary in the block ... I think there were two burglaries in my block. But I haven't had anything happen in my house, I've got the hand of God on my house. (Kaishia, black British young person, 19, Crowford)

These comments highlight how important it is for young people to live in an area where they have a support network comprising family and friends. Those who felt less secure tended not to have this safety net and were clearly isolated; moreover, living in an area that had become notorious for its social problems and heavy police presence compounded their fear of crime.

Substance misuse

Substance misuse is popularly associated with some minority ethnic groups, though they continue to be under-represented among known populations of drug users (Fountain *et al.*, 2003). However, recent research on drug use among Asian young people reported an upward trend in the use of Class A drugs, namely heroin and crack/cocaine (Bennetto, 2000; Rashid and Rashid, 2000; Barn, 2002).

For many young people, engaging in risky behaviour and experimenting with substances is part of the process of growing up, which marks the transition from adolescence to adulthood. At the time of collecting the data, nearly three-quarters of young people reported the use of alcohol and cigarettes during the previous month. However, while alcohol was consumed only occasionally by the majority (52 per cent), tobacco was smoked 'daily' by 42 per cent and 'often' by 16 per cent. Figure 10 illustrates the use of alcohol and cigarettes among the various ethnic groups, and highlights that white and mixed parentage young people were more likely to drink than any other groups, and that white, mixed parentage and Caribbean young people were most likely to smoke 'often'.

Figure 10 Use of alcohol and tobacco during the previous month, by ethnic group (*n* = 260, missing = 1)

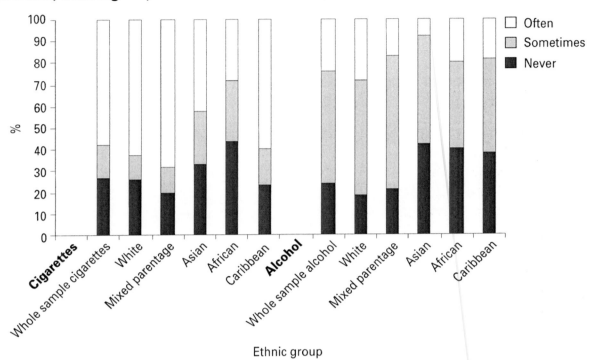

Ethnic group

The use of illegal substances was not widely reported by the young people in our sample. This may be due to the fact that data were collected via the LCT, though anonymously, and some young people may have felt too exposed (see Chapters 1 and 2 for further details). Moreover, certain aspects of individuals' lives, such as drug taking, sexual behaviour or financial status, may be under-reported as 'socially undesirable' (Bradburn *et al.*, 1983). Nevertheless, 46 per cent of the sample had smoked cannabis in the last month. We observed that a small percentage of young people reported taking other substances 'sometimes', such as ecstasy (14 per cent), crack/cocaine (5 per cent), heroin (2 per cent) and other drugs (5 per cent), which included LSD, amphetamines and aerosols. Only a small minority reported frequent use of these illicit substances. We found some geographical variation in the use of these drugs among the young people in our sample; they primarily came from Petersfield and Heatherton (*p* < 0.01).

Figure 11 highlights the use of these substances among the various ethnic groups. We found that about half of the Caribbean, mixed parentage and white young people had smoked cannabis during the previous month. With the exception of Asian young people, all the other groups used ecstasy, though white people used it more often than other groups and also more of them did so.

Figure 11 Use of substances during the previous month, by ethnic group
(*n* = 235, missing = 26)

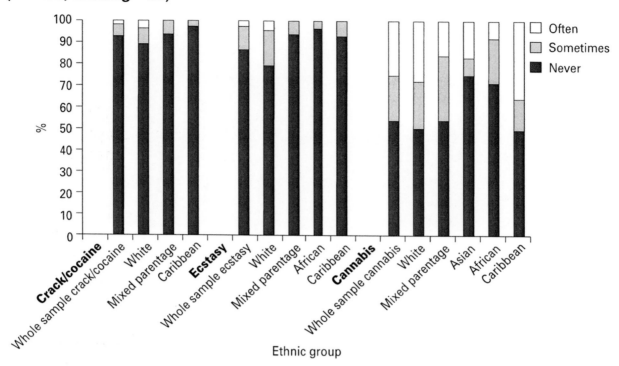

Ethnic group

We also see that a higher proportion of white young people used crack/cocaine during the previous month and took them more often. White young people also reported taking a variety of other drugs such as heroin, LSD, amphetamines and solvents. Interestingly, none of the young people from other ethnic groups reported the use of these latter drugs.

We examined differences in risky behaviour among males and females, and found that an equal proportion of males and females never consumed alcohol during the month, but, while females had the propensity to drink more recreationally than males, males tended to drink more often. Moreover, a higher proportion of females never smoked cigarettes during the month compared to males, though those who smoked did it on a daily basis. Males were more likely to have taken ecstasy and smoked cannabis than females.

During the interviews a number of respondents made reference to cannabis use on a regular basis, indicating that this was a safe pastime. The majority of this group held strong views about the use of Category A drugs, making it clear that these were substances they would not consider taking. Smoking cannabis was primarily to cope with everyday problems and worries:

> I tend to worry about things that it's not worth worrying about ... and it
> makes me want to light up ... you know ... I smoke weed so you know
> what I mean, just to relax my head so that I start to think about whatever.
> Until when it has come up again ... smoking may be used ... um,
> smoking weed is ... um, making me sort of forget things.
> (Charlene, black Caribbean young person, 20, Harwood)

> ... you do find that a lot of foster children do go into drugs. I have been
> into drugs but not heavy ones. You feel that you should cope but you get
> into drugs or into fights. That's how you cope with things. And when you
> get older you realise that and you stop.
> (Cecille, mixed parentage young person, 18, Petersfield)

On a positive note, many young people showed a great deal of insight about their
drug use and why they had now stopped using drugs. Factors such as the wrong
crowd, 'sexual naivety', relationship difficulties, loneliness and stress were commonly
expressed.

Young people in care are said to be at considerable risk of getting involved in
unprotected sex (Corlyon and McGuire, 1997). Our findings show that drugs and
alcohol also played a part in such situations, and research shows that sexual activity
and pregnancy are also linked to 'high-risk' behaviours such as alcohol and drug use
and aggressive behaviour (Valois *et al.*, 1999). Young people often craved love and
affection, and for some stability in their life. Turning to drugs was described as a path
to these states of being, or as a way of dealing with difficult situations:

> The majority of them have ended up on drugs, prostituting, things like
> that. I'm not going to say I haven't ... like I've done escorting when I was
> in care because of the money that you're getting, you can't live on £5 a
> week, I'm sorry you can't. Do you know what I mean? So I had to do
> escorting when I was actually in care, and then from that you get on the
> drugs and everything.
> (Lucy, mixed parentage young person, 16, Petersfield)

> I never took drugs like cocaine, heroin in the past. I did smoke like
> marijuana ... for like ages. I drunk a lot of alcohol you know. I gave them
> both up about a year or so ago ... I was actually completely I would say
> sexually naive ... I actually craved love and attention from someone, you
> know.
> (Veronica, black Caribbean young person, 20, Heatherton)

In our interviews, young people's lack of awareness of the dangerous effects of illegal substances was of concern. Although almost two-thirds of our quantitative sample reported receiving some help and advice on drugs and alcohol, it seemed that young people found themselves exposed to harmful illegal substances, and were often ill-equipped to handle the situation:

> I knew about marijuana because my dad used to smoke it. But nothing else. I went to a training session on alcohol awareness and they told you about units and all that stuff. I found that quite helpful. But stuff like drugs I didn't really know because at one stage I go out to a nightclub and there was one instance when my drink come back and I was spinning around. But my friend told me later that somebody was going around putting stuff in people's drinks. I never realised but the week before I must have had it because my head was spinning, I had cold sweats and I was lost. Never again.
> (Anthony, black Caribbean young person, 21, Petersfield)

The role of foster carers in raising awareness of drugs was highlighted by some young people. They were appreciative of such help and advice:

> Mostly she was telling me about crack, to be aware of it, there's a lot of young people taking it, so she told me to watch out for the friends I keep and don't take drinks – open can drinks – or smoke something that someone gives you. She's just telling me, when I go out, buy my own drink or, if someone buys me a drink, make sure I watch what they do with it before I drink it, she used to warn me about it.
> (Frances, African young person, 19, Petersfield)

We wanted to gauge the level of awareness among young people about accessing help and information on substance use, and we found that the majority knew of at least one agency working with problem drug use (63 per cent). Their knowledge included national or local agencies dealing with drugs or alcohol, which ranged from the helplines such as the National Drug Helplines, or Alcoholics Anonymous, their local hospital or the GP or counsellor, their social services or social worker, or information resources such as local brochures or local projects. A small percentage of young people (8 per cent) reported having sought help with a drinking or drugs problem.

Drug culture and poor neighbourhoods

As mentioned above, the interview accounts of young people show that they often found themselves living in neighbourhoods that they considered to be unsatisfactory. Problems of crime, drugs and violence were highlighted by the young people:

I don't really bump into them I keep myself to myself. Downstairs in the very first flat there are drug addicts there and they drink a lot. I don't associate with them. I just keep well away. I just go to work, come home, have a bath and go to bed or listen to my music. I don't really talk to next door, if I see them on the street I'll say hi but I won't have a conversation. I don't like the look of them.
(Cecille, mixed parentage young person, 18, Petersfield)

… there's a lot of people … boys, young boys, making so much noise, driving and playing loud music and smoking drugs. Don't really feel safe.
(Frances, African young person, 19, Petersfield)

Summary

This chapter has illustrated the extent of risky behaviour among young people and their experiences of becoming victims or perpetrators of crime. Our findings show that, while alcohol was consumed by the majority only 'sometimes' (52 per cent), tobacco was smoked 'daily' by 42 per cent and 'often' by 16 per cent. The use of illicit drugs among care leavers was also considerably higher than among their peers.

Involvement with crime as a victim or a perpetrator was a key focus for the study. We found that almost half of our sample had engaged in criminal activity and over two-fifths reported having been the victims of crime. African and Asian young people reported under-involvement on both counts, while white youngsters reported the highest involvement in crime as perpetrators.

Involvement in risky behaviour such as drug taking and crime could be understood to be a result of many contributory factors including poor housing and homelessness, neighbourhood and peer culture, lack of motivation, boredom, poverty and so on. Young people in our study showed a remarkable insight into their own problems and those of their peers. Efforts to work with such knowledge and understanding are important to equip young people to be better skilled in dealing with difficult situations.

7 Race, ethnicity and the care experience

This chapter explores three important areas of concern – young people's experiences of racism and discrimination, their understanding of racial and ethnic identity, and the response of social services in dealing with diversity and racism.

Experience of prejudice and discrimination

Our quantitative study employed the broad terms of prejudice and racism to explore young people's experiences of unfair treatment. Our findings suggest that most young people reported needing little or no help in dealing with prejudice and discrimination. Only 6 per cent reported that they needed help and assistance to deal with prejudice and racism (see Chapter 9). Asian and Caribbean young people reported needing more help in this area than other groups (10 per cent Asian, 9 per cent Caribbean, 6 per cent mixed parentage, 4 per cent African and 4 per cent white).

It is important to note that needing help cannot be equated with actual experiences of prejudice and racism. The accounts of these youngsters document 'in-care' and 'post-care' experiences involving overt and covert discrimination.

In the main, respondents' accounts of prejudice and discrimination related to their post-care experiences. However, a few talked about their care experiences to suggest that they had either been subjected to racial prejudice and discrimination, or that the lack of appropriate racial/cultural input during care had rendered them incapable of dealing with racism:

> I was living in white care homes as well and they stereotypically thought you know just cos I was black I was going to know about West Indian food. You know it didn't matter that … I could have been an African person, but as far as they were concerned a black person is West Indian. I am, but … do you know what I mean, it was just stereotypical.
> (Alexia, black British Caribbean young person, 23, Heatherton)

Some young people felt strongly that the care system had not adequately equipped them with a sense of their roots, and it was this deficit that was perceived as problematic in trying to deal with prejudice and discrimination:

> … even though in the care system there's all this anti-discrimination and equal rights policies and all that, but even though that's in effect people I don't think within the social services really know how to implement that

into the young person's life. I mean all right you might put a picture of a
black person up on the wall but that isn't giving you your roots.
(Marco, mixed parentage young person, 23, Heatherton)

A number of young people talked about their experiences of racism in employment
(see Chapter 5). Others described how they were affected by subtle racism on a daily
basis, for instance feeling overly scrutinised when entering large department stores.

> I was in a shop recently to return something I had purchased. I didn't like
> the manager's attitude and when I complained he said this is typical of
> 'you people'.
> (Louise, African young person, 22, Harwood)

Asylum-seeking young people who were uncertain about their legal status acutely
felt the impact of racism and negative stereotyping on a daily basis. Also a young
mother (expecting her second child at the time of interview) expressed concerns
about her daughter growing up surrounded by racial intolerance, which she herself
suffered from.

Although, in the main, respondents' experiences of prejudice and discrimination
related to race and ethnicity, those interviewed were invited to share any other
experiences of oppression. Two young men alluded to the discrimination they had
encountered because of their sexuality and the general homophobia that existed in
society:

> Sometimes you look back and you think oh this is what happened. Is it
> because you are black, gay, whatever? Sometimes people said things
> and they don't realise what they have said until they have said it. An
> example was this person who works in social services said to me I have
> never seen a black gay man, you know the way they put it across. I could
> understand if they said you are the first black gay man I have met, but it
> was the way they put it across.
> (Anthony, Caribbean young person, 21, Petersfield)

In our interviews with young people, we explored the strategies and techniques they
employed to challenge and/or combat prejudice and discrimination. Some young
people reported that they regularly challenged the type of behaviour they regarded
as based on ignorance or malice. However, on the whole, respondents were willing
to ignore what they perceived to be covert manifestations of discrimination, feeling
that this did not have a direct impact on their well-being and that to protest would not
make the slightest difference to people's conduct:

> Well I just ignore it … I used to fight, whereas now I just ignore it cos I
> can't be bothered with it … I mean what's the point … it's not going to
> solve anything at the end of the day.
> (Lucy, mixed heritage young person, 16, Petersfield)

For other young people, it was difficult to deal with racial abuse and taunts. An African young person, who had arrived in Britain at the age of seven as an asylum seeker and had been looked after for ten years, reported needing help and advice on how to manage his anger. This young man's father died during the conflict in Somalia and his mother was still in Africa. It was evident that there were difficult emotional issues arising from the traumatic experience and the separation from his family and community. The racist abuse he had experienced living in his current neighbourhood had exacerbated his situation:

> I'm settled in the community, but it's just the racial abuse that I get which I
> think can never make me settle properly. There are some things in life
> which are unchangeable.
> (John, African young person, 17, Crowford)

While appearing conversant with the concept of equal opportunities, only a few of those interviewed were familiar with the equal opportunity policies being operated by their respective local authorities. Others were somewhat cynical about their impact and application:

> Equal opportunities policies are rubbish; you will always find a token
> someone, somewhere.
> (Chantelle, black Caribbean young person, 20, Harwood)

Accounts of young people suggest that very little work had been carried out by social services to address prejudice and discrimination during the stages of preparation and after-care support. There were some examples of good practice. One young person advised us of a specific shift in the practice and ethos of her local authority, referring to an increased awareness among foster carers and the difference a new service designed to improve the life chances of children and young people from minority ethnic communities had made. In another interview, a young man spoke appreciatively of the guidance he had received from staff while residing in a children's home:

> Basically now social services have made a big issue about anyone that's
> an ethnic minority, there's hair and skin care stuff provided if they want it.
> So that's good. So things have definitely improved from what I have seen.
> (Focus group, Veronica, black Caribbean young person, 20, Heatherton)

Respondents' accounts suggest that efforts have been made by particular practitioners to raise young people's awareness of discrimination and its possible manifestation, though there is no sense of any systematic work having been carried out with young people to help them develop mechanisms to cope with the impact of this.

Racial and ethnic identity and the care experience

There is growing evidence to suggest that 'ordinary' minority ethnic young people living with their own families do not experience problems and concerns about their racial and ethnic identity (Tizard and Phoenix, 1993; Fatimilehin, 1999; Barn and Brug, 2005). However, there is conflictual evidence concerning the identity development of minority ethnic young people in care and leaving care (First Key, 1987; Ince, 1998; Robinson, 2000).

Existing literature addressing the situation of minority ethnic children and young people in the care system has identified important concerns around racial and ethnic identity (First Key, 1987; Ince, 1998; Barn, 1999). A range of key factors, including transracial placements, being brought up in rural, predominantly white areas and the lack of positive input around race and ethnicity, have been identified as causes of concern. Minority ethnic young people being brought up in their own birth families, in residential homes comprising minority ethnic and white staff, and in multiracial areas are found to be confident and comfortable about their racial and ethnic identity (Tizard and Phoenix, 1993; Fatimilehin, 1999; Robinson, 2000). It is believed that young people in these situations receive good, positive and appropriate racial and ethnic socialisation messages from their parents and carers, leading to a good understanding of self and group ethnic identity as well as an awareness of racial oppression and the coping strategies to confront racial prejudice (Stevenson, 1995).

Caribbean, African, and Asian young people

The desire to belong, to fit in, to not be assigned a marginal identity was in evidence among the young people in our study. For black Caribbean young people, the self-label of 'black' and 'British' carried an important significance. These young people, while recognising that their parents or grandparents originated from the Caribbean islands, wished to express a strong identification with the label 'black British'. This was designed to serve the purpose of forging their own identity (different from their parents), but also gave them a sense of ownership to the land of their birth – Britain. It signified the contextual and fluid nature of identity (Hall, 1992):

> I'm black British, I was born in England ... I'm an English person, I'm
> British. You don't have to be white to be British.
> (Kaishia, black British young person, 19, Crowford)

The complexity of identification with own ethnic group and/or nation was in evidence
with regards to Asian and African young people. Both groups expressed a strong
identification with their ethnic group culture and felt that this provided an appropriate
individual identity. The significant religious and cultural differences of the Asian group
from the dominant white society played an important role in reinforcing difference. In
situations where Asian young people reported positive racial and ethnic socialisation
within the care system, there was evidence of strong individual and group
identification (Ghuman, 2003). One Asian young man typifies this experience:

> I am Indian ... I love my religion. It has its good points and bad points. At
> the end of the day I don't want people picking on me, name calling me,
> because at the end of the day I like it.
> (Vijay, Indian young person, 17, Heatherton)

Many of the African young people in our sample were born in Africa. They identified
with Africa as their birthplace and felt a strong attachment:

> I see myself as African, because I was born there ... in school there were
> lots of races and in debates I was always complaining about colonialism
> and stuck up for Africa.
> (Mohammed, African young person, 21, Crowford)

Racism is regarded as a powerful influence in highlighting difference and marginality.
Interestingly, some minority ethnic young people described having become more
aware of their difference in a context where their racial and ethnic difference
identified them as 'outsiders', as the 'other'. One respondent described how her
minority status became more 'marginal' when she moved out of London to a
predominantly white university in the north of England.

> I think it's because you know I went to a place where there were really no
> black people, which was really tough coming from London ... When I'm at
> university, me and my black friends, we always say we represent black
> people, because these people don't know what black people are about.
> They've never been around black people, so, whether we like it or not,
> walking, talking, eating, we are representing the black race.
> (Lakisha, African young person, 21, Benton)

The absence of role models to nurture and sustain an awareness and appreciation of one's culture was often expressed during the interviews. Many of the respondents advised us that they could not identify any major influence in this area and it was evident that several young people had no real understanding of this concept. By contrast, a young person explained that she had been assimilated into the British way of life to such a degree that she was not sure how she would relate if placed within a community of Eritrean people (country of origin):

> I've never lived at home, I think culturally I'm 'Britishfied'.
> (Yasmin, African young person, 19, Benton)

Some young people made a connection between cultural mores and values and place of origin. The different approaches to parenting upheld by people born in the Caribbean and those of Caribbean heritage but born in Britain were highlighted. It was also felt that Africans had a more clearly defined value base than people from Europe. Significantly, those who presented as fairly knowledgeable about their cultural background had strong links with either their families or local members of the community from their country of origin:

> An influence on my culture is having been brought up in this family ... It's very important for me to know my own culture. I'm always asking what's going on now, if they're having a ceremony.
> (Vijay, Indian young person, 17, Heatherton)

Our study shows that most young people of Caribbean, African and Asian background held their racial and cultural identity to be an important component of themselves. They expressed pride in their cultural heritage and vocalised the importance of a sense of belonging. Significantly, when compared on identifiable factors of risk and concern, it is evident that the majority of these young people did not fall into the risk category. They were brought up in multiracial areas; many were placed in families that were racially and/or culturally similar to themselves and reported receiving appropriate racial/cultural socialisation by their carers.

Mixed parentage and white young people

The concepts of racial and ethnic identity had little resonance for some white and mixed parentage young people. Respondents found it difficult to relate to or discuss meaningfully what constituted a sense of self or what enabled one to develop an identity.

It is argued that, where 'whiteness' is the norm, white young people may not be required to think about their position in society and thus racial and cultural questions of 'where do I belong?' are not common. Recent evidence suggests that consideration should be given to the ways in which white young people conceptualise and locate themselves in a racially ordered society (Nayak, 2003).

In this chapter, we have suggested that minority ethic young people experience the process of ethnicisation where their racial and cultural identity is marked as different in relation to the dominant group (Phoenix, 2004). The issue of belonging is said to be of particular importance for those of mixed ethnicity. Researchers and practitioners have concerned themselves with various questions such as: can they identity with both (in some cases multiple) groups?; do they suffer rejection from both (multiple) groups?; are they at the periphery of each ethnic group, or do they identify with one or both/multiple group(s)? (Tizard and Phoenix, 1993; Fatimilehin, 1999).

In our interviews with white young people, we learned that two of the four white people we interviewed could, in fact, be described as 'mixed parentage' background, in that their parents came from two different ethnic groups. A mixed parentage young man of Asian/white background who had had no direct or indirect Asian influences in his life described himself as white. It is important to recognise the significance of the notion of 'passing for white' (Piper, 1992). Thus, the labelling of difference can take place only if the difference is recognised. In this case, this young man recalled no real difficulties in passing off as white:

> I feel myself to be white British, but my real dad was Indian. I haven't
> seen him for ages, and my mum is British. So it's quite a difficult category
> to fit into.
> (David, 'white' British young person, 17, Benton)

A young woman who had described herself as white in the postal questionnaire stated that, although she identifies herself as white, her father is in fact a Romany gypsy. She maintained some contact with her father and reported that she had learned a few things about the Romany gypsy culture:

> I am white, I'm a white person, do you know what I mean? But I've got
> that bit of culture in me, and it's not necessarily a race … well it is a race,
> but I'm white.
> (Joanne, 'white' young person, 21, Leyford)

This young woman was herself a mother to a mixed parentage four year old, but perceived her daughter to be also white. In response to a question about the upbringing of her daughter, and exposure to her racial and cultural background, she felt that she lacked the skills and competence to do this as far as the child's Caribbean background was concerned:

> It's like it's not down to me to do that, because I don't know nothing about that, so it's down to her dad … Because he says she's black, you see, and I'll say she's white cos she looks white.
> (Joanne, 'white' young person, 21, Leyford)

Most of the mixed parentage young people in our study were of Caribbean and white parentage and represented a complex picture reflecting the current debates around mixed ethnicity (Fatimilehin, 1999; Prevatt-Goldstein, 1999; Alibhai-Brown, 2001). Some mixed parentage young people defined themselves as black, while others were vehemently opposed to ethnic categorisation, maintaining that this had resulted in a process of labelling individuals without recognising their right to self-definition:

> Confused! Confused would be my identity, I don't know. Every time I see that question I don't know what to put because I'm three different things … Well I am quarter Jamaican, quarter Spanish and half English, whatever that makes me.
> (Chris, mixed heritage young person, 19, Petersfield)

It is not surprising that young people who have been separated from their family and have had limited opportunities to deal with issues of self-identity should express bewilderment, confusion and anger at society's approach to the ethnic categorisation of individuals. What should not be overlooked is how best to achieve reinforcing young people's identity without imposing a construct that leaves a young person feeling that only part of their heritage is being acknowledged.

Many of the mixed parentage young people in our study had been placed in white or Caribbean families. Almost half of the sample were placed in white families, while a third were placed in Caribbean families (see Chapter 3). Those brought up in white families recalled experiences that had been tantamount to 'identity stripping' (Ince, 1998):

> I feel that, from being brought up in care when I was really young, I lost out … I didn't really have an identity, cultural or any, I mean one of the places I was put into they changed my name and everything so a lot of my identity was taken away and it was white folk I was living with, so it was like there weren't no positive black role models or nothing. So I did have identity problems if it weren't for going to live with like a few of my

family members. I think it was that that brought me closely in touch with
my cultural roots, and from then it's like I know who I am now, I like the
black side to me. Obviously I'm mixed race so I've got white and black,
but I identify with my black roots.
(Robin, mixed parentage young person, 17, Heatherton)

Some young people from a mixed background showed clarity about what they
perceived to be their primary identity – that of a black person. This was largely as a
result of being defined as such by 'others', or the positive input of relatives and
carers (Fatimilehin, 1999; Howorth, 2002). The significance of these statements
cannot be overstated:

It is important because it's part of your life really … it's just like, even
though kids that are mixed race, if a white person was to see me they
wouldn't shout 'Oh you half breed' they'd shout 'You fucking nigger'
wouldn't they. They wouldn't shout 'Oh whitey, you've got white in you'.
(Focus group, Marcos, mixed heritage, 23, Heatherton)

My gran is Jamaican and she was the first black person we lived with …
Before I lived with her I didn't think of myself as black, I saw myself as
white. But when my gran told me about my granddad I thought I'm proud
of my colour. I am mixed race but I class myself as black.
(Cecille, mixed heritage young person, 18, Petersfield)

It was evident that mixed parentage young people who had been placed with
minority ethnic relatives and carers found this to be a positive experience. This was
described as a significant influence in their construction of the 'black' identity. It is
important to note that these young people had had minimal contact with their white
relatives, but they acknowledged their white background.

Social services' response

Given the legal requirements to incorporate race and ethnicity into decision making for
children in need and those looked after, (Children Act 1989, section 22 [5] [c]), and the
broader local authority duties to combat racial discrimination and disadvantage and
promote equality of opportunity (Race Relations Act 2000), we sought to explore the
ways in which social services were attempting to undertake this work.

Ethnic monitoring and wider policy framework
In attempting to understand the rationale and framework for the identification and
addressing of minority need, we were keen to show how this was being

operationalised in the agencies. As local authorities are now required to provide the ethnic breakdown of children looked after, we found that all of our agencies were able to demonstrate the existence of such information. However, the ethnic breakdown of care leavers was not readily available in all agencies. And the conflation of some groups, for example, African and Caribbean as black, was not helpful in determining specific needs. Because many African young people in our study were asylum seekers, it is important that the ethnic monitoring data reflect their situation so that appropriate help can be targeted.

The London borough of Benton maintained a good management information system and there was evidence to show that data were being collected for a purpose, that is, to identify need and gaps in provision, and to seek to improve service provision. For example, it was during a data evaluation exercise that the Leaving Care Team in Benton came to realise that its educational budget was under-used by some ethnic groups, namely Caribbean and white young people (see Chapter 4).

Practice and provision can be said to be governed by a policy framework. Although the wider legal framework, mentioned above, is the principle influence, local authorities do develop their own policies to target specific needs and concerns. Our study shows that only one local authority reported such policies relating to minority ethnic care leavers:

> There is a policy statement that has been drawn together by Heatherton
> in meeting the needs of black and dual-heritage children looked after.
> This encapsulates the local authorities' duties and responsibilities around
> black and dual-heritage children looked after.
> (Black senior officer, Heatherton)

> I have to say that apart from monitoring the different ethnicity of young
> people … We haven't taken that step further.
> (White manager, Crowford)

Ethnic matching

In other agencies, staff demonstrated an understanding and awareness of some of the key issues around 'ethnic matching' of workers and care leavers, assessment forms, and specific social work interventions and ethnicity. However, there was an absence of a policy framework, suggesting the potential for a fragmented approach. Responses regarding specific and/or distinct approaches to working with minority ethnic young people or requests for information describing how racism, culture and identity were addressed as part of the preparation process were vague and generally non-committal.

The importance of ethnic matching of social worker and young person was recognised by agencies, and it was made clear that agencies would attempt to meet individual requests:

> I'm not aware of any specific measures although black young people are likely to be the majority in this borough. If a young person requested a black social worker that provision would be made.
> (White senior practitioner, Harwood)

Interestingly, the majority of young people expressed no real preference for social workers from their own ethnic background. On the whole, young people were concerned about the overall quality of worker and their investment in the relationship, as well as their ability to involve them in decision making and treat them with respect. However, having a minority ethnic after-care worker was important for some young people:

> I didn't appreciate having a white after-care worker, not because she wasn't any good, but because I wanted someone who would keep it real.
> (Focus group, Alexia, Caribbean young person, 23, Heatherton)

> I think that it's a positive thing to have a black social worker. They don't take any rubbish and they tell you how it is out there for you as a black person.
> (Focus group, Faye, Caribbean young person, 17, Petersfield)

The complexity of matching clients and workers was highlighted by the agencies. Importantly, a competency approach was considered crucial, whereas the background of the worker was secondary. The need for adequate and appropriate training to ensure that staff were equipped to deal with clients from a range of backgrounds was expressed. The involvement of care leavers was considered to be vital:

> … our view is that it is everybody's responsibility to be knowledgeable about issues to do with black children. It shouldn't be left to the black staff to meet the needs of black children. All staff should meet the needs. So it is about developing different strategies and services to train staff adequately to meet those needs. One of the ways we are attempting to do that is that we have recruited some ex-care leavers to deliver a rolling programme of minimum standards for black children.
> (White manager, Heatherton)

We have two young women who are African and it almost felt a
coincidence that they were allocated to Musa … who's an African guy
and that's working well … but, I wouldn't say that was a policy, that was
the way we allocated.
(White senior practitioner, Petersfield)

Although there were no specific policies, our interview accounts suggest that some
ethnic matching may be taking place. This could be due to the fact that, if allocation
were based on skill and competence, then implicit recognition could be given to the
fact that a black worker might be the most suitable person to deal with such a case.
At a practice level, this has a number of service implications, since it may be that
skin colour is mistakenly equated with 'race' expertise (Laming, 2003). Apart from the
risk of over-burdening black members of staff, such practice prevents white staff from
developing skills and knowledge in the areas of race and ethnicity.

Specific services and interventions

As mentioned above, only one of the six local authorities that participated in our
study had a specific policy regarding service provision for minority ethnic young
people. This was also the only local authority that reported a specific and targeted
service for minority ethnic youngsters. The complexity of undertaking work in this
area was highlighted by the black practitioner heading this service and this is
perhaps an indication of why other agencies are reluctant to get involved in such
interventions:

… flawed really just on the basis that if they have been in local authority
care for any length of time and they have been in a transracial placement
… their access to black individuals or black communities will be quite
limited. So you've got your work cut out anyway just in terms of what sort
of things do you think that you should have or could have had in
replacement. A lot of them haven't got a clue, so there is obviously a
process of education that has to take place even at the stage of them
coming into contact with us at 16.
(Black Caribbean senior officer, Heatherton)

In the other research sites, no specific projects or groups were reported to be in
existence. However, managers and practitioners emphasised an individualistic
approach, which attempted to identify and meet needs and concerns of young
people. The pathway plan combined with a mindful approach to ethnicity was
considered to be a useful tool. It is interesting that practitioners highlighted the need
for identity work. With the exception of Heatherton, where a number of young people

mentioned a specific focus on issues of race and ethnicity, the accounts of young people suggested that only a few recalled any work on identity by their personal advisers:

> It's a matter of the social workers doing that work on an individual basis with young people and then using outside resources if they feel there is a need for specific counselling or refer to a particular organisation … we are moving towards doing some specific work around identity.
> (White manager, Benton)

> I suppose one of the things that goes throughout a young person's life in care would be identity and family issues. And I suppose that would lead into the pathway plan for young people.
> (White manager, Crowford)

There is a risk that a lack of specific focus on race and ethnicity in the assessment and review forms can lead to an omission of key information. This concern was expressed by a senior black practitioner:

> … it's in the Assessment and Action records as well, there are specific sections around identity in there. So you're supposed to be able to use that creatively to deal with that. Now if you do use it creatively that's fine, but if you use it as a straightforward thing you miss it out completely, you can just skip over things. Which is why I think the forms are not good at all.
> (Black Caribbean senior practitioner, Benton).

The involvement of service users in the design and delivery of services is increasingly recognised within the personal social services. Our study shows that some of the authorities were engaged in efforts to consult young people. This ranged from a proactive stance involving clear rationale and strategy to one that was governed by the efforts of young people themselves:

> One of the things we are doing presently is to try and actually get young people through the door to access the black resources service drop in, which then creates a space for them to share experiences and ideas around what is the most appropriate way of delivering quality services to them.
> (Black Caribbean senior officer, Heatherton)

Summary

Our study demonstrates the complex ways in which young people choose to define their racial and ethnic identity, and highlights some key influences in shaping these identities. It is evident that cultural influences, experiences of prejudice and discrimination, geographical context and ethnicity, and positive racial socialisation messages from relatives and carers are important in the development and formation of racial and ethnic identity in young people.

As a result of being exposed to racism, some minority ethnic young people had given more thought to their identity than some of their mixed parentage and white counterparts. We found that Caribbean, African and Asian young people were generally more self-assured and had a strong belief in their individual and ethnic group identity. On the other hand, mixed parentage young people presented a variety of experiences reflecting their particular context and backgrounds. Accounts of young people reveal that very little work had been done by social services to explore the ways in which young people in general express and experience their racial and ethnic identity.

Our study shows that, with the exception of Heatherton, which had made creative use of Quality Protects money to address racial and ethnic identity issues, agencies seemed to feel it was sufficient to employ a multiracial staff group and did not feel that work of this nature needed to be informed by a policy framework. Despite referring to the use of pathway planning and the needs assessment process as tools to incorporate ethnic sensitivity, these departments were on the whole reliant on the competence and commitment of individual workers. Few agencies were using existing legislation or initiatives like Quality Protects to enhance their service provision in this area.

8 Preparation and after-care support

Preparation for leaving care and after-care support are highly important stages to ensure that young people are adequately equipped with the necessary life skills to cope with living independently following their discharge from care. Previous research has emphasised the need for the preparation stage to be an ongoing process rather than a single event (Stein and Carey, 1986; Biehal *et al.*, 1995; Broad, 1998).

To facilitate the transition to self-sufficiency, social services are under a duty to empower young people with the necessary practical skills and emotional support during the preparation and after-care stages (Children Leaving Care Act 2000). Research evidence suggests that:

> … practical and social skills need to be developed gradually through care and that this process should be supported, participatory and holistic in approach.
> (Biehal *et al.*, 1995, p. 144)

Given the limited attention paid to issues of race and ethnicity, our study aimed to explore these by focusing on the perspectives of young people and professionals. This chapter examines the help and support provided by Leaving Care Teams on and following exit from care, and areas of unmet need identified by care leavers living in the community. The findings suggest that multiple disadvantage experienced by young people requires serious attention to prevent marginalisation and social exclusion.

Help and advice received before leaving care

One of the key concerns of this study was to establish the impact of race and ethnicity on use of and access to service provision. It is important to note that, with regard to the key socio-economic areas of housing, employment and finance, our study found few ethnic differences in help and support received by young people (see Figure 12). Asian young people reported higher levels of help in a range of areas, but caution needs to be exercised because of the small number of Asian young people in our sample ($n = 12$).

In a question about levels of satisfaction with their social worker, there were again no key ethnic differences. However, a gender difference was observed. Overall, a significantly high proportion (two-thirds) of the young people expressed satisfaction with the help received from their social worker. We found that males were generally more satisfied than females. Given that two-fifths of our female sample were teenage mothers, it is possible that their needs and concerns were greater, reflecting lower levels of satisfaction with social services (61 per cent of females expressed satisfaction with their social worker compared with 77 per cent males).

Figure 12 Type of help and advice received before leaving care, by ethnic group (*n* = 250, missing = 11)

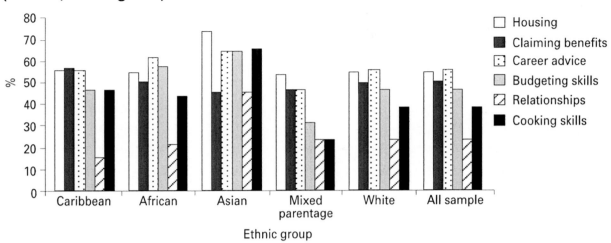

Overall, our quantitative findings show that about half of the group reported receiving help and advice with housing, claiming benefits, budgeting skills and careers before they left care (Figure 12). Worryingly, many young people recalled not having been given necessary help and support. For example, more than half of the group reported little or no help with budgeting skills. In a question about what help would you have liked before leaving care, 'budgeting skills/general management skills/ understanding bills' was reported as the primary concern.

While a focus on housing and benefits is crucial, our findings show that other areas of life skills also require attention. Only four out of ten young people reported receiving help with cooking skills and only two out of ten recalled support with family and personal relationships.

Our study sought to elicit what young people perceived as appropriate preparation. For the majority of those interviewed, preparation for leaving care was not an ongoing process but was said to commence at the age of 16. However, for some young people, this input began a few months before they were due to leave. Being swept away by the fast pace of the transition, from being looked after to living on their own, was a shared experience among many. Some also noted that they had been given little time to adapt to the new situation, which was accompanied by feelings of loneliness and isolation. Indeed, over half of the young people in our sample lived alone (see Chapter 5):

> ... the initial leaving care bit I didn't have ... I mean there wasn't any preparation for that. There was no one to talk to me about what my options were.
> (Veronica, Caribbean young person, 20, Heatherton)

Some young people were quite critical of the lack of support in general they had received from the local authority, but spoke highly of the input they had received from foster carers and semi-independent placements. One young woman in particular from Harwood maintained that her placement at such a unit had given her the opportunity to take responsibility for practical and domestic aspects of her life.

The significant contribution of foster carers and residential units was acknowledged by all social work professionals. Young people were said to be made aware of this service and its role in helping them to achieve transition from care and achieve independence.

The role of foster carers in helping to prepare young people for leaving care was a common theme in the accounts from young people. They felt that this had been an ongoing process whereby they were being equipped to learn basic skills such as cooking and cleaning, and being organised and self-disciplined. They also felt emotionally supported and continued to maintain contact with the carer after leaving care:

> … well my foster parents they started preparing me beforehand, before my social worker, because they *[social services department]* didn't start preparing me until the year I was leaving … I had good foster parents and they prepared me a lot, more than the social workers. They don't really prepare you. But like my foster family, I'm still on the phone to them now, even though they've stopped fostering me now, but we still stay on the phone and I'll go and meet them and everything, but they prepared me a lot without me even realising.
> (Kylie, white British young person, 20, Benton)

> Me and my foster mum kind of get on well so she showed me what type of food I should be eating and we do sit down and talk about girl stuff, you know the changes I ask her about it and she explains it. If I have a problem with cooking myself a suitable meal, she'll sit down and write a diet for me.
> (Frances, African young person, 19, Petersfield)

It was interesting to note that young people seemed to make a clear distinction between social services help and help provided by foster carers and staff in semi-independence units. Comments made by young people during the qualitative interviews revealed that foster carers in the main were regarded as totally independent of social services. It is also important to note that some young people experienced severe placement disruption while in care. The lack of similar positive foster experiences for these young people is a concern.

There was some recognition of the limitations of social services provision. However, most social work managers and practitioners held the belief that they provided a comprehensive service that commenced formally at 15:

> Well I'd say we've got the accommodation, we've got a financial policy that supports them … so I'm quite happy; we've got a reasonable infrastructure.
> (White, senior manager, Leyford)

> At 15-and-a-half we go to a young person's statutory review to tell them about the team and what to expect, also to establish what preparatory work had already been done in a residential unit or with foster carers.
> (White senior practitioner, Harwood)

> What we aim to do is to implement the legislation in relation to care leavers, which can sometimes be very challenging … but what we do here is undertake our work with every young person as an individual and we attempt to look at all their individual needs and we attempt to be realistic in what we can offer to them as individuals.
> (White senior practitioner, Petersfield)

Professional ideologies of need and assessment seemed to be at odds with young people's views and experiences. As documented in our findings, over half of our sample reported little help and support in the key area of budgeting skills. This was also evident in the interview accounts of young people.

Several young people maintained that the quality of preparation was inextricably linked to the calibre of a young person's personal adviser. This view was particularly prevalent in Harwood where respondents participating in a focus group expressed strong feelings about this matter. As far as they were concerned, the fact that they had been well supported and informed about their entitlements had nothing to do with the actual system, but was due to the individual commitment and effectiveness of their allocated workers. In contrast, respondents from Benton and Crowford maintained that their negative experiences were a direct result of an unfair and inconsistent system and its practices. Young people's views about inconsistent and unfair practices were often about money and principally about leaving care grants, which varied in and between local authorities:

A minute ago, I was outside and saw this bloke writing a list of things he needed and how much money. He said he wanted like £300, the social worker said that would be possible. But nothing like that has been done with me.
(Yasmin, African young person, 19, Benton)

I've heard of situations where young people in similar positions have received totally different amounts from social services. I mean, what's that about?
(Louise, African young person, 22, Harwood)

After-care support

The development of specialist provision in the form of Leaving Care Teams is generally regarded as a positive step in the co-ordination of leaving care policies and services (Biehal *et al.*, 1995; DoH, 1997; Broad, 1998). It is also recognised that, where young people have experienced poor planning and support while they are looked after, it will be difficult for a specialist service to provide adequate compensation (Wade, 2003).

Previous research suggests that specialist services can help to improve outcomes for young people leaving care (Biehal *et al.*, 1995). Specialist schemes have been found to be successful in helping young people find appropriate accommodation, and in providing support to help them maintain their homes and to develop life skills. They have tended to be less successful in improving outcomes for young people in the area of education and employment, at least until recently, and for young people with very poor social networks and relationship skills, for whom overall outcomes tend to be poor. However, the informal and flexible approach to service delivery adopted by many schemes may help to reduce the risk of social isolation, through a mix of support and social activities, and to encourage young people to return for help when they need it (Biehal *et al.*, 1995; Stein and Wade, 1999).

Findings from our quantitative data show that higher proportions of young people reported receiving help and support with housing and benefits after leaving care than before (68 and 61 per cent compared to 54 and 50 per cent respectively before leaving care, see Figures 12 and 13). Following their exit from care, as young people were now having to deal with real-life situations concerning money and housing, it is likely that help and support received in these areas had a more realistic applicability and meaning.

Figure 13 Help and advice by LCT after leaving care, by ethnic group
(*n* = 254, missing = 7)

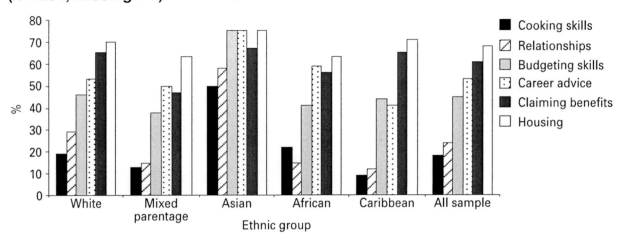

With regard to other areas of need, it is still a concern that a sizeable proportion recalled not having been given necessary after-care support (see Figure 13). For example, almost half of the group reported inadequate help with budgeting skills.

Our study found some gender differences in help and support in such areas as claiming benefits and careers advice, with young women being less likely to seek help in these two spheres. In an analysis of the policy and provision documents of the care and after-care services made available to young people by all the research sites, it was stipulated that these services were geared primarily to integrate young people in their local community by providing stability. In Petersfield, for instance, the team aimed to provide advice and direct support with day-to-day issues such as homelessness, education, training and employment. The emphasis on life skills such as building and maintaining relationships, and cooking was less pronounced.

Identified areas of need after leaving care

Our study sought to identify areas of need with which young people still required help and support now that they were living in the community and were being helped by their Leaving Care Team (LCT). Our findings show that most young people still required help with money matters (67 per cent) and housing (60 per cent). This is not surprising since over a third of the group had experienced homelessness, and 16 per cent reported living in temporary and unsuitable accommodation such as bedsits, bed and breakfast and hostels (see Chapter 5). Given that less than a quarter of the sample were in work, it is again not surprising that almost two-thirds of the group expressed the need for help with money matters.

Figure 14 shows the ethnic group similarities and differences in a range of areas from housing and employment to cooking skills. Our findings suggest that there are no discernible differences between minority ethnic and white young people, but there is an overall pattern showing areas of greatest need. We can see, for instance, that housing, employment and financial matters are a concern for most young people. Other areas such as cooking skills, and dealing with prejudice and discrimination are lower down on young people's list of priorities. This is understandable given that food and shelter are the two basic needs affecting young people's survival on exit from care.

Asian young people expressed the greatest need in education, employment, cooking skills, and dealing with prejudice and racism. A number of Asian young people went into further or higher education on leaving care. This suggests that education was an area of importance for this group and they set out to seek social services' help. As previously stated, Asian young people had spent the least amount of time in care. Thus, they had entered care as adolescents and were perhaps more vocal about expressing their needs and concerns. Interestingly, Asian young people also reported higher levels of satisfaction with their social worker.

Our findings show that, for many young people, a considerable degree of disadvantage is already in place by the time they become involved with a Leaving Care Team. Placement instability, lack of contact with birth family/community, lack of racial/cultural input and poor educational outcomes (see Chapters 5, 6, 7 and 8) are experienced by young people in varying degrees. Leaving Care Teams are imbued with the task of preparing young people to become independent and cope 'on their own', but clearly this must be influenced by young people's early experiences. Young people can benefit fully only if previous disadvantage is taken into account.

Figure 14 Areas of help most needed since leaving care (*n* = 246, missing = 15)

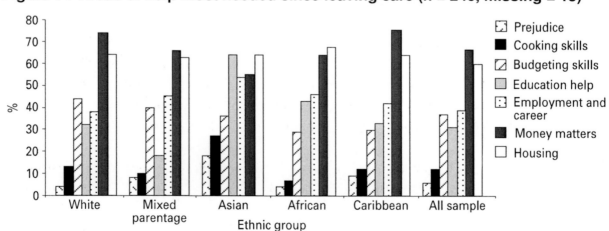

The areas of identifiable need remain the basic ones around money and housing. While almost two-thirds of the quantitative sample reported receiving some help in these areas from the Leaving Care Teams, they also expressed an ongoing need for further support after leaving care. Our quantitative findings show that money matters and budgeting skills are an important area of concern for young people. Interview accounts lend further evidence to illustrate the ways in which lack of budgetary skills hindered young people's attempts to manage their finances on a daily basis.

Money, how to manage it and its significance on a daily basis was a common feature in all the interviews, and, in line with our quantitative data, young people identified this area as their most serious concern. All those interviewed had experienced financial hardship:

> I think the most thing that, um, I needed help with really was financial area … because you don't really know how expensive things can be.
> (Chantelle, Caribbean young person, 20, Harwood)

> But in terms of helping me to budget and manage money and all that I didn't really have much support.
> (Veronica, black young person, 20, Heatherton)

> My spending habits are really bad. I have three years' rent arrears yet I still went out and bought a leather sofa.
> (Louise, African young person, 22, Harwood)

In terms of actual budgetary skills, our qualitative data reveal that there was little difference between those in receipt of benefits and those who were regularly assisted by social services. Both these groups expressed feelings of powerlessness and a sense of low self-worth with their financial predicament, and believed that this was a specific need that the preparatory process had failed to address:

> I remember I got a letter about budgeting and I went to one of their lessons and it didn't really help me. They think that budgeting is about buying cheap food and that's not what it's about. It's about being able to buy everything that you need without putting yourself in debt.
> (Shanice, black British young person, 19, Benton)

In contrast to the young people, the majority of professionals interviewed were of the opinion that young people were routinely appraised of their financial entitlements. They felt that, while there had been some anomalies pre the C(LC)A, a fairly comprehensive package based on a needs assessment informed by the new legal categories introduced by the legislation was now in place. Significantly, all professionals interviewed were confident that young people were appropriately supported in techniques to manage their money and three of the sites advised us that budgetary skills were covered as part of a leaving care preparation group, contrasting markedly with sentiments echoed by users, which were noted earlier in this chapter.

Our study shows that the majority of young people in our sample were not in regular contact with their families. In our interviews, only one respondent reported receiving a regular allowance from a relative. Because of the constrained relationships between young people and their families, the majority of respondents preferred not to look to their families for financial assistance and were more likely to ask friends for small loans.

Young people reported getting into severe debt and rent arrears, which resulted in homelessness as they lost their flat or bedsit (see Chapter 5). Other young people found themselves in desperate situations where they needed immediate financial help. In the absence of supportive family and friends, one young mother reported approaching social services for help but to no avail:

> I'd run out of nappies ... I phoned her *[after-care worker]* and asked if I could have some money to get some ... but she read me the Child Protection Act basically, because I didn't have what I needed for the baby.
> (Laura, mixed parentage young woman, 19, Leyford)

A major concern for young people was the lack of after-care support. The social services' expectation that, on being placed in their own accommodation, a young person should be able to live independently was a shock for many young people. Our study shows that a third of the young people in our sample left care at the age of 16; and another fifth left at 17. Also, in comparison with other young people, white young people left care earlier. For example, white young people were four times more likely than Caribbean young people to leave care at the age of 16 (41 compared to 11 per cent):

> ... it should be illegal, and it's disgusting to put people in flats at the age of 16 because they're children.
> (Joanne, white young person, 21, Leyford)

At the time of the interviews, each participating site advised us that they were in the process of updating their leaving care policies and procedures in accordance with the requirements of the C(LC)A 2000. All professionals appeared satisfied with the framework that this legislation had provided to the service, although most of them maintained that, since they had already been operating within the ethos of the Act, their services had not needed to undergo any major changes. Nonetheless, the majority of professionals consulted felt the legislation had enhanced the service offered to young people, particularly pathway planning and the defined role of personal adviser:

> I feel we are meeting all the objectives of the Act ... we've introduced pathway plans and personal advisers and ... have made inroads in terms of tracking and keeping in touch with young people.
> (White senior manager, Leyford)

> I think that, prior to the C(LC)A, many young people were leaving at 16 because they felt they wanted to, and as responsible corporate parents we weren't doing enough really to encourage them to remain where they were.
> (White senior practitioner, Petersfield)

Although many young people in the quantitative survey had expressed satisfaction with their social worker, their experiences about personal advisers were not always positive. The role of the personal adviser was described as fundamentally flawed; it was argued that staff did not engage with young people on a personal level:

> You can ask sometimes for personal advisers but you know the way they're operating, from my experience, it's just like they're the mediator for financial services, that's all.
> (Craig, mixed heritage young person, 16, Leyford)

Leaving care planning

Although professionals were fairly confident about the manner in which pathway planning was administered and the individual approach employed by workers, this was not the experience of the majority of young people who were interviewed. Evidence gathered from the qualitative interviews highlights this as an area young people were unhappy about. One individual who made reference to his pathway plan was evidently unclear about the status of this document. While the majority of respondents were aware that plans had been made regarding their transition, their role in this process emerged as minimal:

> ... upon my 16th birthday I was introduced to the Leaving Care Team and we done something called a pathway plan. And I just got questions like:

what can I do?, what do I need help with? For example, do you need help with budgeting?, can you make an appointment at the doctor's? So I told them everything honestly and nothing really come of it really.
(Craig, mixed heritage young person, 16, Leyford)

Most of the time they seemed to have this perception that because you are in care everybody else is better than you. They think they can walk all over you and treat you the way they think best. Do what I say or just get on with it.
(Focus group, Alexia, Caribbean young person, 23, Heatherton)

I didn't feel I had a choice in any of it. I didn't get on with my social workers.
(Emma, white British young person, 18, Petersfield)

There were a handful of positive experiences regarding the planning process and the majority of these were made by young people from Harwood. The accounts of these young people indicate the importance of a participatory approach involving the dissemination of information, working in partnership and valuing young people as citizens:

I think there can be quite a lot of information on what is going on. They made sure they spent time with me so that I understood what was going on.
(Semhar, African young person, 19, Harwood)

My social worker was really good, she made sure I was involved in everything.
(Chantelle, black Caribbean young person, 20, Harwood)

Sometimes I would get fed up of the whole thing, you know plans, reviews, etc., then my social worker would remind me that this was about my life.
(Louise, African young person, 22, Harwood)

Rights and entitlements

A number of the young people interviewed did not have an understanding of their rights and entitlements as care leavers or an awareness of their current legal status, and revealed that they had been given very little information about this. A consequence of not being appropriately informed about one's entitlements as a service recipient is that young people are rarely in a position where they feel empowered, which may lead them to conclude that their choices are restricted. In one instance, a young person felt he did not receive the correct information about semi-independent living and therefore rejected this option because he did not fully understand what it entailed:

> … um, I don't think I know too much about my rights … Even though they explained to me about the semi-independence I never got that kind of in-depth of it … I didn't really know what it was. I was a bit scared I didn't understand the actual … term of being there before you move ... So I thought that maybe they could have given me more knowledge on that section because then, I could have probably gone for that and got myself extra prepared for moving now.
> (Semhar, African young person,19, Harwood)

> I never got shown a copy of the Leaving Care Act; I never got told what I was completely entitled to. The only thing I was told was that I was a relevant child, rather than an eligible child.
> (Craig, mixed heritage young person, 16, Leyford)

Young people who are aware of their rights and are furnished with accurate information are in a position to make better-informed choices and emerged as far more proactive and resilient. This was acknowledged by one young person from Harwood, who applauded her after-care worker for advising her that financially she would be better off if she went to university at 18 and did not delay this until she was 21. An illustration of empowering young people is the following:

> I'm very big on knowing what my rights are … In terms of decision making, I wouldn't allow somebody just to make a decision that would change my life without me having any say in it. And if there was any inclination I would be very quick to quote section 20 of the Children Act and all the rest of it.
> (Kaishia, black British young person, 19, Crowford)

Summary

Much has been written about the importance of preparation and after-care support for care leavers. Our study shows that there is a lack of congruence between the perceptions of social care professionals and care leavers. The latter report limited and inadequate assistance in some of the key areas such as budgeting skills, benefits, housing and careers advice. This was found to be the case at both the preparation and after-care stage. Social care professionals reported providing assistance in all these areas.

It is likely that the accounts of both groups represent a situation of reality. Indeed, many young people reported a good relationship with their social worker, and commented on the positive help from foster carers and others. However, they were less sanguine about their level of competence in basic life skills such as budgeting. Social care professionals reported providing help but acknowledged certain limitations such as the unsuitability of housing.

Our study reveals that a combination of poor housing, low income and a lack of budgeting skills can lead some young people to get into debt and consequently to become homeless. The study shows that, without an adequate knowledge base about rights and entitlements, and an appropriate skills base, young people are ill-equipped to manage accelerated social change.

The study also documents that a young person's particular set of circumstances wields a great deal of influence. Those with poor in-care experiences suffer greatest disadvantage after leaving care. Some young people show remarkable resilience and appear to take advantage of the opportunities. It is apparent, however, that a clear and focused approach is crucial at both the preparation and after-care stage to engage young people and help with the transition to independence.

9 Conclusions and recommendations

This study has attempted to fill a gap in research on young people leaving care in England. Although 'leaving care' has received considerable attention in recent years, few studies have focused on care leavers from minority ethnic groups and some of the most influential studies are honest about their failure to recruit from these groups in their sampling (Biehal *et al.*, 1995). This research has also used both quantitative and qualitative data. A questionnaire survey of 261 male and female 16–21-year-old young people included a significant number from minority ethnic groups (44 per cent). Six different local authorities were covered: three London boroughs and three local authorities in the North and Midlands. The London authorities were chosen to reflect a mix of different ethnic groups. One of the northern cities also had a sizeable Pakistani population. Interviews were also conducted with professional workers and their managers so as to gain information on the policies and practices on care leavers.

Disadvantaged transitions

The questionnaire survey enabled the research to examine the situation of male and female care leavers as they are discharged from care – their educational attainments, employment and training careers, housing careers, parenting and household formation and any involvement in crime either as perpetrators or victims. It produced some findings that are, perhaps, counter-intuitive. We know, for instance, that, nationally, people from many minority ethnic groups suffer very significant disadvantage in terms of both the educational qualifications they attain (Gillborn and Mirza, 2000) and higher rates of unemployment (see Barn, 2001). Moreover, when in employment, minority ethnic groups tend to get poorer jobs with lower pay (Ethnic Minority Employment Task Force, 2004). We further know that young people 'looked after' are highly vulnerable and have some of the worst youth transitions outcomes of any comparable group (Biehal *et al.*, 1995; Utting, 1998; DoH, 1999b; SEU, 2003). Combining these, the suspicion has always been that the multiple disadvantages of care leavers who are also members of minority ethnic groups must surely leave members of these groups even more exposed to the risk of poor outcomes. Yet the questionnaire survey undertaken for this research reveals a complex picture of ethnicity and disadvantage.

The evidence presented in earlier chapters indicates that white young people experienced worst outcomes in relation to placement disruption, educational attainment, homelessness and risky behaviour such as the use of illicit drugs. Caribbean and mixed parentage young people were also among those who were at a higher risk of disadvantage; however, there are some useful insights into their particular transitions. For example, while both Caribbean and mixed parentage young people experienced lengthy periods in care, the former achieved greater levels of placement stability in the form of same-race placements. They were also more likely to be living in multi-racial areas. Also, while whites, Caribbeans and those of mixed parentage background experienced high rates of school exclusion, the Caribbean grouping were more likely to go on to college for further study to obtain educational qualifications. However, in spite of this, they still experienced high rates of unemployment. Mixed parentage young people, on the other hand, not only spent lengthy periods in care, but also experienced severe placement disruption and poor education outcomes.

African and Asian groups emerged as two groups who experienced least instability in care and in education. Many of these young people entered care as adolescents and therefore spent a shorter period being looked after. Statistical data collected by the Department of Health (2001b) show that there is a correlation between length of time in care and educational attainment; that is, in general, young people who are looked after for longer periods do educationally better than those looked after for a shorter time. Our findings are not able to support this. We would argue that the length of time in care has to be understood in a wider context of placement and school stability, support from professionals and carers, and personal motivation and confidence. Many of the African and Asian young people had experienced stable care placements, and were less likely to report being excluded from school. Asian young people also reported the highest levels of satisfaction with their social worker (see Chapter 8). It could be argued that these youngsters were able to use the system to their advantage because they had not suffered the same levels of long-term 'in-care' disadvantage and instability as their peers.

The disparate outcomes of these groups are linked to length of time in care, placement and school disruption, and school exclusion experiences. Becoming a parent at a young age may also be a contributory factor in poorer education outcomes and subsequent life chances for some groups. Compared to other groups, whites, Caribbeans and those of mixed parentage may have been so disadvantaged and over such a long period of time before they reach the age at which they leave care that, by that time, the disadvantages prove to be so overwhelming and long-term that this accumulation impacts on subsequent life chances.

Racial disadvantage, prejudice and patterns of cultural support

The quantitative research undertaken helped highlight a number of issues concerning the experience of minority ethnic young people while being looked after, prepared for and eventually leaving care. The qualitative study focused on post care, however, some respondents did comment on both prejudice and discrimination in care, and more specifically that they were not always given appropriate cultural and racial support during placements. For asylum-seeking young people, especially, uncertainty about their legal status and their prospects left them unsettled and highly vulnerable to stereotyping and racism on a daily basis. Yet professional workers commented favourably on the tenacity of asylum seekers in trying to put trauma and adversity behind them and work towards a positive future for themselves.

The research also highlighted particular issues around 'white' and 'mixed parentage' children. Those classified in these two categories included a range of different cultural backgrounds. 'White' included some with an Irish, East European or Romany family heritage. There were several cases of young people who, although self-classifying as 'mixed parentage', also described how they had experienced 'identity stripping', while others described how, much of the time, they had been 'passing for white'. Many had not been exposed to a racial or cultural background that would have given them the skills and competence to try to do anything else. Nearly half had been placed in white families and a third with Caribbean families.

Perhaps surprisingly, only one of the local authorities had a specific policy for service provision for minority ethnic young people or had made a concerted attempt to make equal opportunities issues central to their pattern of provision and sensitive to the distinctive needs of minority ethnic children. This is required by the 1989 Children Act and the Race Relations Act of 2000.

The importance of ethnic matching of the young person with their social worker was recognised by agencies. On the one hand, many agencies reported that, were this to be requested by the young person, then they would comply. Young people, on the other hand, seemed less concerned with ethnic matching than with the quality of the worker. However, young people did comment on the importance of appropriate matching with their after-care worker. This, they thought, was important in increasing the likelihood of them being given appropriate and sensitive preparation and support for independent living. Practitioners, too, commented that some of the assessment and action records used, particularly in the 'transition-planning' process, were sufficiently ambiguous as to lead to the omission of key aspects of information or areas of concern, particularly concerning ethnic identity issues.

Preparation for leaving care

Preparation for leaving care and after-care support has been the subject of significant change under new guidance and regulations accompanying the Children (Leaving Care) Act (C[LA]A) 2000, which came into effect in September 2001. Many of the respondents to the questionnaire survey and those interviewed would have undertaken 'pathway planning' and received support as covered by the Act. The aim of the reforms was to bring the process of moving children 'looked after' to independent living more in line with the experience of other children where the main youth transitions are both protracted and later than in previous decades.

On some of the key areas about transitions, including housing, employment and finance, there were no observed differences between the different ethnic groups in reporting preparation and help. However, while there were no differences, this should not disguise the fact that around half of all groups did not recall help and advice on some of the most basic issues, such as housing, careers, claiming benefits, budgeting skills and cooking. Despite the intention of C(LA)A 2000, many of the sample felt swept along by the fast pace of changes required of them after the age of 16. Many were required to live independently shortly thereafter with little time to adapt. Pathway plans intended to empower young people by encouraging them to enter into dialogue with professional workers in identifying their needs were reported as disappointing. Many thought they were given no choice but to accept unsuitable accommodation or none at all. As well as being disempowering, these 'forced choices' resulted in feelings of isolation and loneliness, often in accommodation and communities in which the young people felt lost and afraid.

Overall, young women were more critical of social worker support than young men and were also less likely to report help and support on claiming benefit and careers advice. There were some differences between the ways in which the different local authority areas arranged such support. The majority of professionals interviewed thought that young people leaving care were routinely appraised of their entitlements and that many of the anomalies that had existed prior to the implementation of C(LA)A (such as very different allocations made through leaving care grants) had now been replaced by a more comprehensive needs assessment. Yet, young people remained concerned particularly about the accumulation of debt and threats to their tenancies, and their inability to be able to avoid this through careful budgeting was a continuing concern. On the positive side, many reported continued support from their foster carers. This was often mentioned as a source of support, albeit often depending on an established good relationship between the young person and foster carer. In this sense, it was based on good will rather than being contractual.

Rights and entitlements

Only in the authority that had an explicit policy on young people from minority ethnic groups were there more systematically positive views expressed on the help and support these young people had received. One key aspect in promoting the welfare of young people is ensuring that they are aware of their rights and entitlements. This is particularly true of care leavers where such knowledge is an important means through which they can self-monitor the implementation of policy and practice, and particularly the guidance and regulation issued on the implementation of C(LA)A, 2000. Yet, there is evidence from this research that many care leavers are given too little information about their entitlements under the Act.

Recommendations

Since this is the first extensive research on minority ethnic care leavers, a number of recommendations arising from the research findings are considered necessary. These are grouped below under two main headings.

General recommendations

- Social services and schools must promote positive educational aspirations for young people in care.

- Local authorities should create employment opportunities for care leavers, offering trainee/apprenticeship positions within the authority.

- A multi-agency approach must be adopted to develop a strategy that ensures young people receive the support they need to maintain tenancies.

- To enable them to make an informed decision, young people should be provided with user-friendly information detailing post-care housing options.

- Family contact is a crucial factor in the development of a young person's identity. Social services departments need to take proactive measures to support young people in sustaining family contact once they leave care.

- Pathway planning should pay equal attention to a young person's capacity to manage independently and leaving care services should invest more time and resources in skill-building programmes. Focused/tailored approaches to budgeting, which take account of different scenarios in which young people may find themselves, are important. Also, follow-up support to settle young people in their new environment would ensure that young people don't feel abandoned and isolated, and are given practical advice that could be applied to their own situation.

■ Young people preparing to leave care should receive up-to-date information about rights, entitlements and service provision. This should take the form of written, audio/visual and other types of media to engage with a diversity of care leavers.

■ Systems in place for measuring the quality of contact with young people should be subject to regular reviews.

Recommendations for minority ethnic care leavers

■ Given the low rates of minority ethnic young people on government training schemes, it is of concern that there is a lack of possible access to routes into employment for these young people. LCTs and the Connexions service need to address this area of concern.

■ Leaving care services should review their policies and practices in the context of the requirements of the Race Relations (Amendment) Act 2000.

■ Leaving Care Teams should work more closely with community-based organisations in order to meet the needs of minority ethnic young people.

■ Race, ethnicity and self-conceptualisation should be formally addressed with all minority ethnic young people as part of the preparatory process.

■ Social care professionals need to develop approaches towards positively reinforcing a young person's racial and ethnic identity.

■ All practitioners should receive training that addresses racial and ethnic identity issues.

■ Given the overt and covert racism experienced by minority ethnic care leavers, social work agencies need to ensure that adequate work is done with young people to prepare them for successfully dealing with this kind of social exclusion.

Notes

Chapter 2

1   Statistics in this section: ONS (2003), Census 2001.

2   Average of Ward Scores: a measure that describes the district as a whole. The district ranking 1 is the most deprived and 354 the least deprived. Department of Transport, Local Government and the Regions (2000), Indices of Deprivation 2000.

3   Statistics in this section: DoH (2002), Children Looked after by Local Authorities Year Ending 31 March 2002; DoH (2002), Key Indicators Graphical System 2002 – data update (ethnic composition of looked-after children).

Bibliography

ABSWAP (Association of Black Social Workers and Allied Professionals) (1983) *Black Children in Care: Evidence to the House of Commons Social Services Committee.* London: ABSWAP

Alibhai-Brown, Y. (2001) *Mixed Feelings: The Complex Lives of Mixed-race Britons.* London: Women's Press

Allen, M. (2003) *Into the Mainstream: Care Leavers Entering Work, Education and Training.* York: York Publishing Services for the Joseph Rowntree Foundation

Barn, R. (1990) 'Black children in local authority care: admission patterns', *New Community*, Vol. 16, No. 2, pp. 229–46

Barn, R. (1993) *Black Children in the Public Care System.* London: BAAF

Barn, R. (ed.) (1999) *Working with Black Children and Adolescents in Need.* London: BAAF

Barn, R. (2001) *Black Youth on the Margins.* York: York Publishing Services for the Joseph Rowntree Foundation

Barn, R. (2002) 'Parenting in a "foreign" climate: the experiences of Bangladeshi mothers in multi-racial Britain', *Social Work in Europe*, Vol. 9, No. 3, pp. 28–38

Barn, R. (2005) *Quality Protects Research Briefings – Race and Ethnicity.* London: DoH

Barn, R. and Brug, P. (2005) *Ethnicity, Mental Health and Young People.* London: DoH

Barn, R., Sinclair, R. and Ferdinand, D. (1997) *Acting on Principle: An Examination of Race and Ethnicity in Social Services Provision for Children and Families.* London: BAAF

Bebbington, A. and Miles, J. (1989) 'The background of children who enter care', *British Journal of Social Work*, Vol. 19, Vol. 19, No. 5, pp. 349–68

Bennetto, J. (2000) 'Drug addiction is surging in the Asian community', *The Independent*, 10 January

Bentley, T. and Gurumurthy, R. (1999) *Destination Unknown, Engaging with the Problems of Marginalized Youth.* London: Demos

Berthoud, R. (1999) *Young Caribbean Men and the Labour Market: A Comparison with Other Ethnic Groups.* York: Joseph Rowntree Foundation

Berthoud, R. (2000) *Family Formation in Multi-cultural Britain: Three Patterns of Diversity.* Working Paper No. 2000-34. Colchester: Institute for Social and Economic Research (ISER)

Berridge, D. and Brodie, I.(1998) *Children's Homes Revisited.* London: JKP

Berridge, D. and Cleaver, H. (1987) *Foster Home Breakdown.* Oxford: Blackwell

BIC (Black and In Care) (1984) *Black and In Care Conference Report.* London: Blackrose Press

Biehal, N. and Wade, J. (1999) '"I thought it would be easier": the early housing careers of young people leaving care', in J. Rug (ed.) *Young People, Housing and Social Policy.* London: Routledge

Biehal, N., Clayden, J., Stein, M. and Wade, J. (1992) *Prepared for Living? A Survey of Young People Leaving the Care of Three Authorities.* London: National Children's Bureau

Biehal, N. *et al.* (1995) *Moving on: Young people and Leaving Care Schemes.* London: HMSO

Bluth, J. and Rugh, D. (2001) 'England', in A. Cherry, M. Dillon and D. Rugh (eds) *Teenage Pregnancy – A Global View.* Westport, CT and London: Greenwood Press

Borland, M. *et al.* (1998) *Education and Care away from Home.* Edinburgh: Scottish Council for Research in Education

Bradburn, N.M. *et al.* (eds) (1983) *Handbook of Survey Research.* New York: Academic Press

Britton, L. *et al.* (2002) *Missing ConneXions: The Career Dynamics and Welfare Needs of Black and Minority Ethnic Young People at the Margins.* Bristol: The Policy Press

Broad, B. (1994) *Leaving Care in the 1990s*. Westerham: Royal Philanthropic Society

Broad, B. (1998) *Young People Leaving Care: Life after the Children Act 1989*. London: Jessica Kingsley

Broad, B. (2003) *After the Act: Implementing the Children (Leaving Care) Act 2000*. Leicester: De Montfort University Children and Families Research Unit

Burgess, C. (1981) *In Care and into Work*. London: Tavistock

Chavalier, A. and Viitanen, T.K. (2003) 'The long-run labour market consequences of teenage motherhood in Britain', *Journal of Population Economics*, Vol. 16(2), pp. 323–43

Corlyon, J. and McGuire, C. (1997) *Young Parents in Public Care – Pregnancy and Parenthood among Young People Looked after by Local Authorities*. Report of Component 1 of Preparation and Support for Parenthood. London: National Children's Bureau

Davies, J. *et al.* (1996) *Homelessness among Young Black and Minority Ethnic People in England*. Sociology and Social Policy Research Working Paper 15. Leeds: University of Leeds, Federation of Black Housing Organisations and CHAR

DfEE/DoH (Department for Education and Employment/Department of Health) (2000) *Guidance on the Education of Children and Young People*. London: HMSO

DfEE (Department for Education and Employment) (1999) *Statistics of Education. Schools in England*. London: DfEE

DfEE (Department for Education and Employment) (2001) *Transforming Youth Work*. London: Connexions, DfEE

DfES (Department for Education and Skills) (2002) *Permanent Exclusions from Schools, England 2000/2001*. SFR10/2002. London: DfES

DfES (Department for Education and Skills) (2003) *Aiming High: Raising the Achievement of Minority Ethnic Pupils, Consultation Paper*. London: DfES

DoH (Department of Health) (1991) *The Children Act 1989 Regulations and Guidance, Volume 4, Residential Care*. London: HMSO

DoH (Department of Health) (1997) *'When Leaving Home is also Leaving Care': An Inspection of Services for Young People Leaving Care*. London: SSI, DoH

DoH (Department of Health) (1998) *Quality Protects: Framework for Action*. London: HMSO

DoH (Department of Health) (1999a) 'Quality Protects', *Transforming Children's Services*, No. 3, November

DoH (Department of Health) (1999b) *'Me, Survive, out there?' New Arrangements for Young People Living in and Leaving Care*. London: DoH

DoH (Department of Health) (2000a) *Quality Protects Management Action Plans: A Thematic Review of Leaving Care Services*. London: DoH

DoH (Department of Health) (2000b) *Framework for the Assessment of Children in Need and their Families*. London: The Stationery Office

DoH (Department of Health) (2001a) *Children (Leaving Care) Act 2000: Regulations and Guidance*. London: DoH

DoH (Department of Health) (2001b) *The Children Act Report 2000*. London: DoH

DoH (Department of Health) (2003) *Commentary: Children Looked after Statistics*. London: DoH

(The) Ethnic Minority Employment Task Force (2004) *Equality, Opportunity, Success. Year 1 Progress Report, Autumn*. London: Ethnic Minority Employment Task Force

Fatimilehin, I.A. (1999) 'Of jewel heritage: racial socialization and racial identity attitudes amongst adolescents of mixed Afro-Caribbean/white parentage', *Journal of Adolescence*, Vol. 22, pp. 303–18

First Key (1987) *A Study of Young Black People Leaving Care*. London: CRE

First Key (1992) *A Survey of Local Authority Provision for Young People Leaving Care*. Leeds: First Key

Fitzherbert, K. (1967) *West Indian Children in London*. London: Bell and Sons

Fountain, J. *et al.* (2003) *Black and Minority Ethnic Communities: A Review of the Literature on Drug Use and Related Service Provision.* London: National Treatment Agency for Substance Misuse

Francis, J. (2000) 'Investing in children's futures: enhancing the educational arrangements of "looked after" children', *Child and Family Social Work*, Vol. 5, pp. 241–60

Garnett, L. (1992) *Leaving Care and After.* London: National Children's Bureau

Ghuman, P.A.S. (2003) *Double Loyalties, South Asian Adolescents in the West.* Cardiff: University of Wales Press

Gillborn, D. and Mirza, H.S. (2000) *Educational Inequality, Mapping Race, Class and Gender: A Synthesis of Research Evidence.* London: Ofsted

Glaser, B.G. (2002) 'Conceptualisation: on theory and theorising using grounded theory', *International Journal of Qualitative Methods*, Vol. 1, No 2, pp. 1–31

Glaser, B.G. and Strauss, A.L. (1967) *Discovery of Grounded Theory: Strategies for Qualitative Research.* Hawthorne, NY: Aldine de Gruyter

Godek, S. (1977) *Leaving Care: A Case Study Approach to the Difficulties Children Face in Leaving Residential Care.* Social Work Papers No. 2. Hertford: Barnardo's

Hall, S. (1992) 'The question of cultural identity', in S. Hall, D. Held and T. McGrew (eds) *Modernity and its Futures.* Cambridge: Polity Press

Howorth, C. (2002) 'Identity in whose eyes? The role of representation in identity construction', *Journal for the Theory of Social Behaviour*, Vol. 32, No. 2, pp. 145–62

Ince, I. (1998) *Making it Alone: A Study of the Care Experiences of Young Black People.* London; BAAF

Jackson, S. (1997) *The Education of Children in Care.* Bristol: University of Bristol, School of Applied Social Studies

Jackson, S. and Martin, P.(1998) 'Surviving the care system: education and resilience', *Journal of Adolescence*, Vol. 21, pp. 565–83

Jackson, S. and Sachdev, D. (2001) *Better Education, Better Futures*. London: Barnardo's

Jones, G. (1995) *Leaving Home*. Milton Keynes: Open University Press

Kahan, B. (1979) *Growing up in Care*. Oxford: Blackwell

Laming, Lord (2003) *The Victoria Climbié Inquiry*. Cm. 5730. London: The Stationery Office

Millham, S. *et al.* (1986) *Lost in Care*. London: Dartington Social Research Unit, Gower

Milner, D. (1983) *Children and Race, Ten Years on*. London: Allan Sutton Publishing

Nayak, A. (2003) *Race, Place and Globalisation: Youth Cultures in a Changing World*. London: Berg

NCB (National Children's Bureau) (1992) *Child Facts*, 25 June

NCH (National Children's Home) (1954) 'The problem of the coloured child: the experiences of the National Children's Home', *Child Care Quarterly*, Vol. 8, No. 2

Phoenix, A. (1991) *Young Mothers*. London: Polity Press

Phoenix, A. (2004) 'Reflections on debates in the study of racism and ethnicity', paper given at the 'Inclusion and Exclusion: Racism and Ethnicity in Research, Policy and Practice' conference, SSRG, 17 May, London

Pierson, J. (2002) *Tackling Youth Exclusion*. London: Routledge

Pinder, R. and Shaw, M. (1974) 'Coloured children in long-term care', unpublished report, University of Leicester, School of Social Work

Piper, A. (1992) 'Passing for white, passing for black', *Transition*, Vol. 58, pp. 4–32

Prevatt-Goldstein, B. (1999) 'Black, with a white parent, a positive and achievable identity', *British Journal of Social Work*, Vol. 29, No. 2, pp. 285–301

Race Relations (Amendment) Act 2000. London: The Stationery Office

Randall, G. (1989) *Homeless and Hungry*. London: Centerpoint

Rashid, H. and Rashid, S. (2000) 'Similarities and differences: working respectfully with the Bangladeshi community', in A. Lau (ed.) *South Asian Children and Adolescents in Britain*. London: Whurr Publishers

Robinson, L. (2000) 'Racial identity attitudes and self-esteem of black adolescents in residential care: an exploratory study', *British Journal of Social Work*, Vol. 30, No. 3, pp. 3–24

Rowe, J., Hundleby, M. and Garnet, L. (1989) *Child Care Now: A Survey of Placement Patterns*. Research Series No. 6. London: BAAF

SEU (Social Exclusion Unit) (2003) *A Better Education for Children in Care*. London: SEU

Small, J. (1984) 'The crisis in adoption', *International Journal of Psychiatry*, Vol. 30, Spring, pp. 129–42

Smith, J., Gilford, S., Kirby, P., O'Reilly, A. and Ing, P. (1996) *Bright Lights and Homelessness*. London: YMCA

Stein, M. (1990) *Young People Leaving Care*. London: Royal Philanthropic Society

Stein, M. and Carey, K. (1986) *Leaving Care*. Oxford: Blackwell

Stein, M. and Wade, J. (1999) *Helping Care Leavers: Problems and Strategic Responses*. London: Department of Health

Stevenson, H.C. (1995) 'Relationship of adolescent perceptions of racial socialisation to racial identity', *Journal of Black Psychology*, Vol. 21, No. 1, pp. 49–70

Sudman, S. and Bradburn, N.M. (1983) *Asking Questions*. San Francisco, CA: Jossey-Bass

Tikly, L. *et al.* (2004) *Understanding the Educational Needs of Mixed heritage Pupils*. Research Report RR549. London: DfES

Tizard, B. and Phoenix, A. (1993) *Black, White or Mixed-race?* London: Routledge

Utting, W. (1991) *Children in the Public Care: A Review of Residential Child Care*. London: HMSO

Utting, W. (1998) *People Like Us: The Report of the Review of the Safeguards for Children Living away from Home*. London: The Stationery Office

Valois, R.F., Oeltmann, J.E., Waller, J. and Hussey, J.R. (1999) 'Relationship between number of sexual intercourse partners and selected health risk behaviours among public high school adolescents', *Journal of Adolescent Health*, Vol. 25, No. 5, pp. 328–35

Wade, J. (2003) *Leaving Care*. Quality Protects Research Briefing, No. 6. London: Department of Health

Ward, L. (2000) 'New Deal "less likely" to benefit ethnic minority youths', *The Guardian*, 11 February

Ward, J., Henderson, Z. and Pearson, G. (2003) *One Problem among Many: Drug Use among Care Leavers in Transition to Independent Living*. Research Study 260. London: Development and Statistics Directorate, Home Office

Wright, C. (1987) 'The relationship between teachers and African Caribbean pupils: observing multiracial classrooms', in G. Weiner and M. Arnot (eds) *Gender under Scrutiny: New Enquiries in Education*. London: Open University/Unwin Hyman

Also in this series

Young Turks and Kurds: A set of 'invisible' disadvantaged groups
Pinar Enneli, Tariq Modood and Harriet Bradley

Young Bangladeshi people's experience of transition to adulthood
Mairtin Mac an Ghaill and Chris Haywood

This publication can be provided in alternative formats, such as large print, Braille, audiotape and on disk. Please contact: Communications Department, Joseph Rowntree Foundation, The Homestead, 40 Water End, York YO30 6WP.
Tel: 01904 615905. Email: info@jrf.org.uk

Life after care